WaxPoetics

Wax Poetics Journal Issue 68 (Winter 2020) is published in the U.S. by Wax Poetics (www.waxpoetics.com). © 2020 Wax Poetics. ISBN 978-0-9992127-7-6. Printed by Lightning Source. All rights reserved. Unauthorized duplication without prior consent is prohibited. • Front cover of Digable Planets from the Pendulum Records promo photo by Guzman. Back cover photo of P.M. Dawn by Chris Carroll/Corbis. • Founded by Andre Torres, Dennis Coxen, and Brian DiGenti. Editor: Brian DiGenti. Associate Editor: Thomas McClure. Editorial Ambassador: Andrew Mason. Designed by Wax Poetics. • European Publishing and Brand Partner: holt&co. (www.holtandco.net). • Contributing Writers: Joey Altruda, A. D. Amorosi, Travis Atria, Michael A. Gonzales, Josh Lewellen, Allen Thayer, Layne Weiss, Frank White. Contributing Photographers: Chris Carroll, David Corio, Daniela Federici, Antonio Luis, Sheila Pree, David Redfern, Nina Schultz, Betty Tichich, Mario Luiz Thompson, Dean Van Nguyen, Cathrine Wessel, Frank White, Philip Woo.

CONTENTS

Origins (*Reachin'*)	**004**
The System	**010**
Raymond Scott	**016**
Susaye Greene	**024**
P.M. Dawn	**034**
James Mason	**048**
Novos Baianos	**056**
Cerrone	**070**
Rap-A-Lot Records	**086**
Digable Planets	**102**
Frank White	**114**

ORIGINS

A sampling of the sphere of influence for *Reachin' (A New Refutation of Time and Space)*, the debut album of the Digable Planets.

Rebirth of Slick (Cool Like Dat)

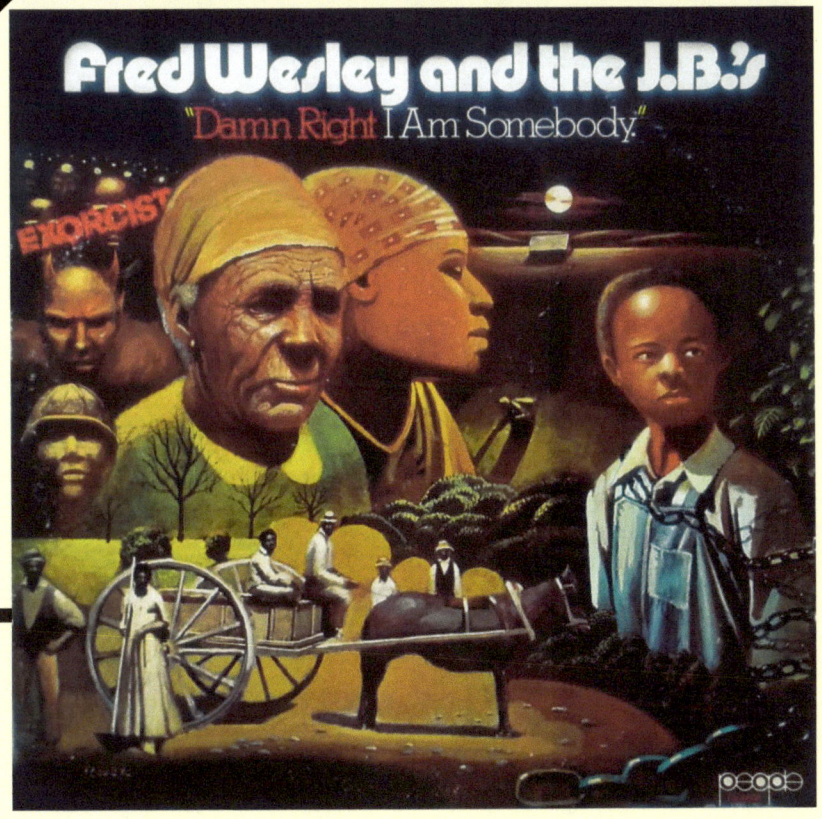

It's Good to Be Here

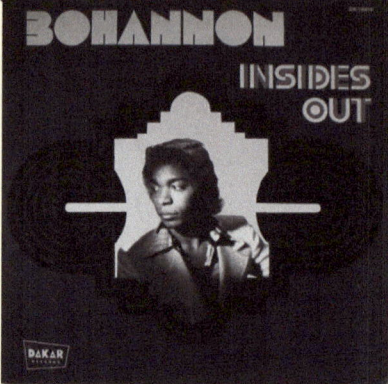

Pacifics

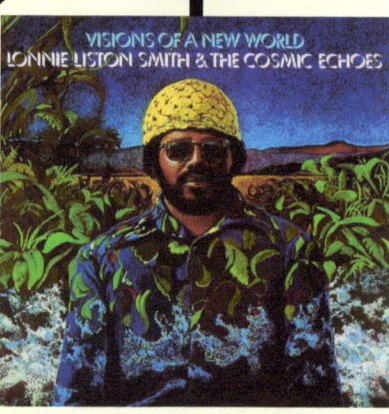

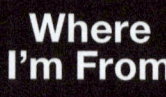
Where I'm From

What Cool Breezes Do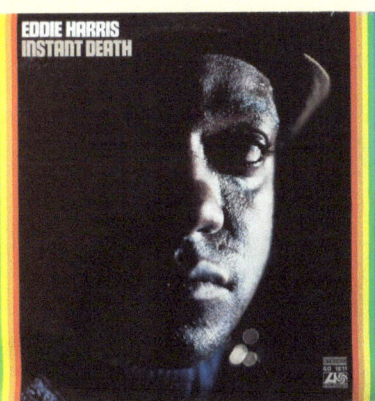

Time and Space (A New Refutation Of)

Jimmi Diggin' Cats

 **La Femme Fetal**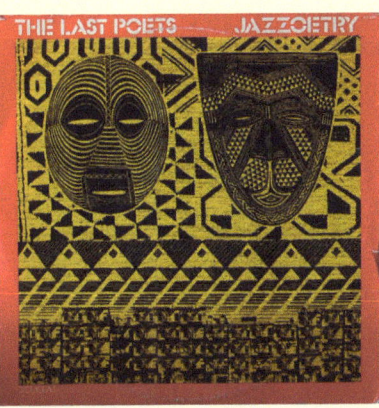

Escapism (Gettin' Free)

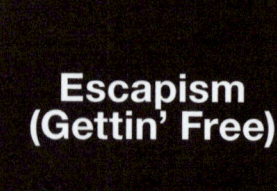

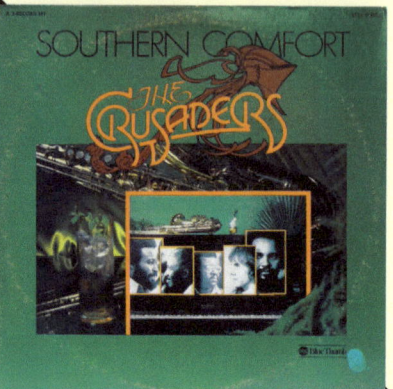

Appointment at the Fat Clinic

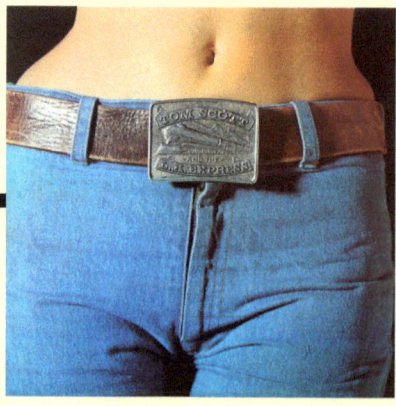

 **Nickel Bags**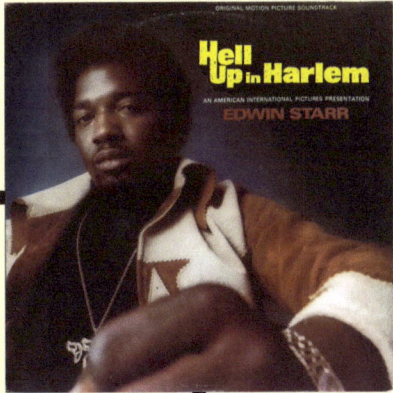

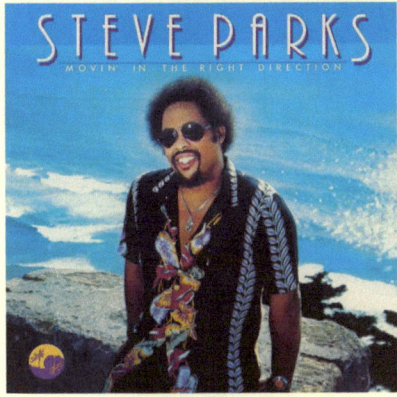  

Swoon Units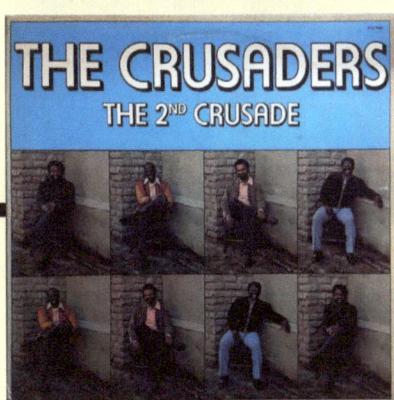

 **Examination of What**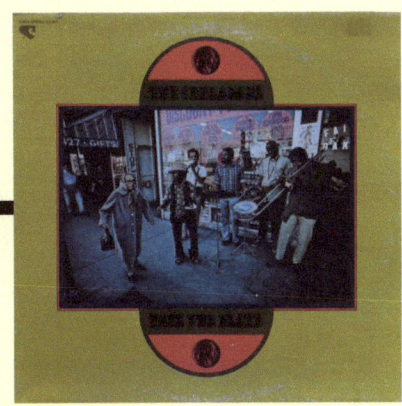

Shadow Revolution

Drummer Bob Lamb and guitarist/vocalists Bob Wilson and Dave Carroll made a 180 degree turn from their U.K. guitar-rock outfit the Steve Gibbons Band and formed a keyboard-driven trio named the System, creating a small batch of synth tunes once shrouded in mystery.

by Josh Lewellen

"It's either the best record you've ever heard, or the worst."

These words, spoken to me by musician and producer Bob Lamb, are in reference to *Logic*, the one-off album of an English band known as the System. Released in 1983, the record absconded to the coterie of obsessives and collectors almost instantaneously, original pressings hidden under the cover of myth in all the decades since. And, as Lamb half lets on, it is among the greatest sound recordings to emerge from the 1980s.

(opposite) From the inner sleeve of the System's *Logic* LP. Photo by B.T. Jag T.P.

Comprised of three former members of the Steve Gibbons Band—namely Lamb (the band's drummer) and guitarist/singers Bob Wilson and Dave Carroll (who would all take up the keyboard for the new project)—the System both appeared and vanished with equal haste. Between 1981 and 1983, the group released a single containing the songs "Sixty Watt Pearl" and "Fergie," and then the record the System's myth is staked on in *Logic*. Though a longtime fixture among audiophile cognoscenti (*Logic*, to these ears, ranks among the best-produced albums in existence), the synth-pop of the System remained largely unearthed for the better part of thirty years until the lauded Dutch reissue outfit Music from Memory put out a compact but indispensable EP, documenting some of the album's peaks while also including a particularly notable unreleased track, "Find It in Your Eyes."

For those bearing even a passing familiarity with the Gibbons Band—a rock-and-roll band through and through, one which spent years in the 1970s opening for a fellow Polydor act in the Who (due in part to Pete Townshend's endorsement of SGB to manager Bill Curbishley)—the mention of synth-pop would justifiably arouse a great deal of confusion, considering the not-so-storied record of former pub rockers vaulting across that particular sonic border; but the result of this left-field mutation marks what is perhaps the apogee of the genre, achieved mere moments into its commercial dominance yet wholly precluded from partaking in its spoils.

Though Lamb is quick to point out that the work produced by this trio bore no connection to the disbandment of their previous group—with the songs "Styletto" and "Feather in the Dust" even being holdover compositions from the Steve Gibbons Band period—the sheer disparity of sound between the two entities would at least indicate, rather loudly, a yearning for less well-trodden musical avenues among Lamb, Carroll, and Wilson. Starting out the project operating out of Lamb's own recording studio for an apartment (earlier put to use as the staging grounds for UB40's debut album, which, thanks to a producing credit, granted Lamb the finances needed for a warehouse studio to complete the project in question) and aiming to self-release the album on his label, Romantic Records, the three positioned themselves to create what Lamb simply termed "a pleasing record."

"I mixed the album in two long days, with the help of a couple of bottles of whiskey and some of the other thing," says Lamb. "I have to admit that I was responsible for it becoming the strange and evocative record that it became, but I remember it was a very pleasurable experience. I was well aware that, at times, the keyboards completely overshadowed the guitar, but, to me, that was the essence."

Upon hearing *Logic*, one raises the immediate question of chronology. The record is unremitting in its melding of dense keyboard layers, world-beating percussion, alternating vocalists who occupy ground just outside the sphere of mechanical precision, instead possessed by off-kilter languidness and ambivalence, and streaks of Wilson's light-bringing guitar. The result is, as Lamb also notes, a strange record, but the exact outline of its strangeness shares the same fog that envelops its vocalists. As of the time of this writing, the System unleashed *Logic* thirty-five years ago—it would be every bit as transfixing were it released today, or thirty-five years from now. That it failed to make so much as an innocent nick in the public or critical consciousness of then and now perhaps speaks to this conundrum, its being of the time and epochs ahead, nearly impervious to that oft-used descriptor: dated.

According to Lamb, "The recording process for *Logic* was split between the two studios, which made it somewhat different to usual sessions. The bedsit eight-track work was a writing and arranging time, and the new studio was the finishing period, with more tape space available, enabling us to work on ideas and experimentation. The two instrumental tracks were put together from start to finish in the larger place. They were mainly me messing around with keyboards, late at night in my spaced-out time. I was preplanning a particular midnight-blue mood for the record to keep the flow rolling from start to finish."

The music contained between those vinyl grooves skates with ease through visions of nighttime missions and cosmic

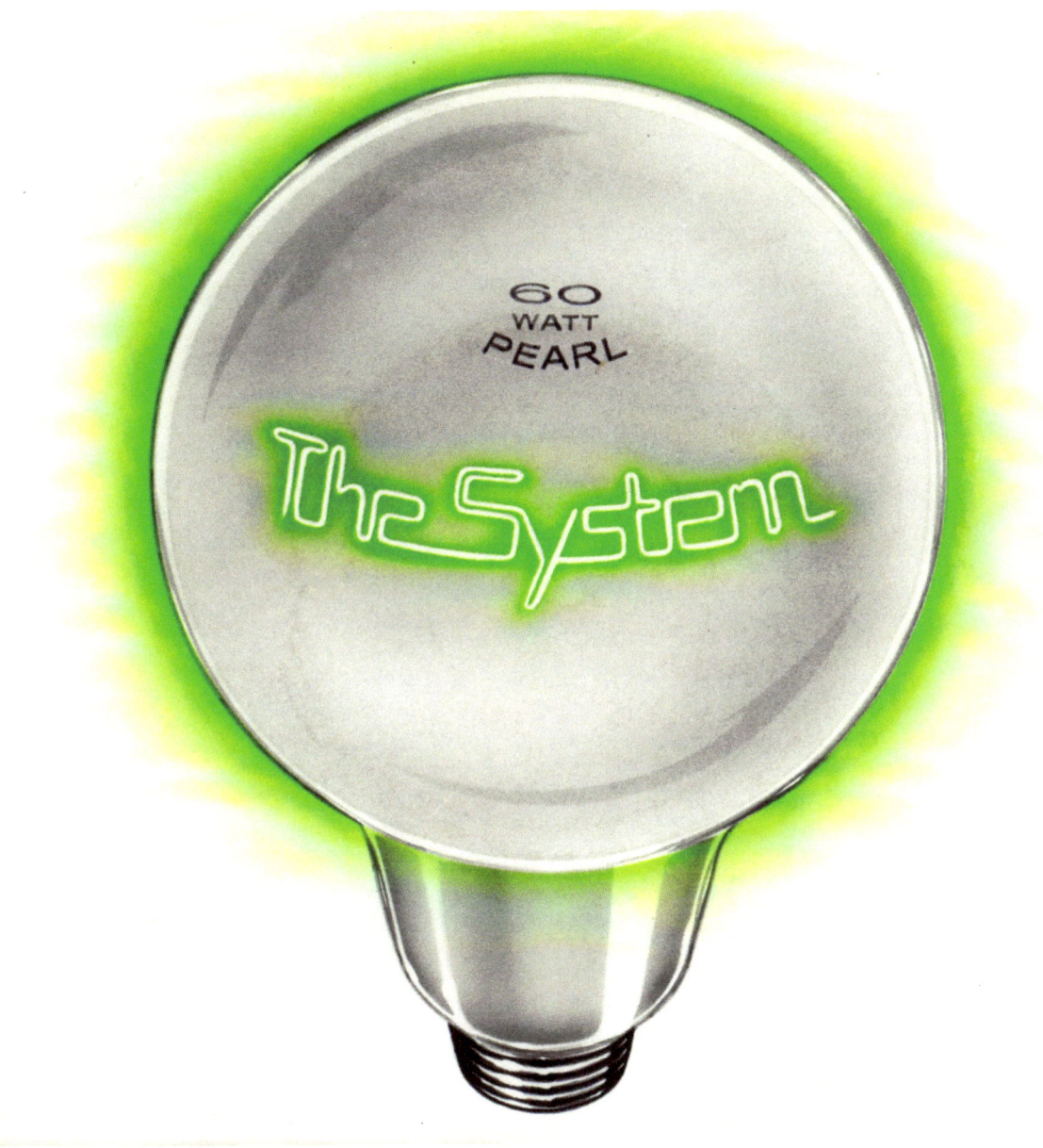

Artist: The System
Record: "60 Watt Pearl" b/w "Fergie" (7-inch single)
Label: MCA Records (U.K.)
Catalog: MCA 731
Release year: 1981
Produced by: Bob Lamb
Written by: Dave Carroll

Artist: The System
Album: *Logic*
Label: Romantic Records (France)
Catalog: 574042
Release year: 1983
Produced by: Bob Lamb
Written by: The System
Guitars, Keyboards, Voice: Bob Wilson and Dave Carroll
Percussion, Keyboards, Voice: Bob Lamb
Sleeve photos by: B.T. Jag T.P.

intentions, evenly possessed of gale-like synth lines and voices game for both smoked-out caverns and whiskey-informed moon landings. The virile opener "Your Love (Will Stay in My Heart)" marks the first in this series of nocturnal shuffles, fittingly accompanied by the sensation of a nighttime free fall in the instrumental "Vampirella" and, later, the sound of deep-space suspension in "Pendy! You're in Some Awful Danger." Needless to say, the midnight mood alluded to by Lamb remains intact until the closing seconds of the album, and this unity is just as apparent lyrically as it is musically, with undeviating verses marking these forlorn highways like headlights of concern.

The unassailable centerpiece of the record, "Almost Grown," is a salvo of kinetic force, a spiritual inheritor of the same desperation coursing through that most spellbinding of musical lonely nights in Del Shannon's "Runaway." Sung by Wilson—who also laid down the crucial keyboard hook that pierces through massive walls of synthesizer and percussive sound (on an album replete with studio flourishes, the production here reaches an altogether different plane)—the closing number of the record's first side hurtles headlong through the dark causeways and astral spaces put in place by the preceding minutes of cosmic tones, and when Wilson and company howl the line "nights away from home" again and again out into the ether, one can't help but wonder if this distance apart should be measured in interstates or light-years.

While "Almost Grown" shows the System at their official pinnacle, its unofficial companion in the originally shelved "Find It in Your Eyes" only further reinforces the trove of riches birthed in Lamb's pop laboratory. Containing some absolutely lewd bass and a culminating guitar solo that could just as easily be mistaken for something off *Purple Rain*, the mere fact that it went unreleased and presumably unheard for over three decades is perhaps even more perplexing than the scarcity of recognition surrounding *Logic* itself.

In their renewed search for joy and pleasure in the act of creating, Lamb, Wilson, and Carroll found catharsis and then some. Late hour though it may be, their work, a document of the strange beauties that can be found in even stranger places, may yet find its way into that sacred realm of the windows-down moonlit soundtrack, where those space-bound sounds will sustain all the itinerant souls rumbling down unknown passages toward a deeper shade of night. ●

(*above*) Rhythm section of the Steve Gibbons Band and trio of the System: (left to right) Bob Lamb, Bob Wilson (front), and Dave Carroll. Photo by John Shaw, cropped from the back cover of 1978's *Down in the Bunker* (Polydor) by the Steve Gibbons Band.

Light Year Prophet

Synthesizer innovator and composer Raymond Scott captured the imagination of a crate-digging corner of the hip-hop community decades after recording jingles like the Dilla-sampled "Lightworks."

by Layne Weiss

In the mid-2000s, James Yancey aka Jay Dee aka J Dilla sat in a hospital bed in Los Angeles making what would be his final album, *Donuts*. Arguably the most popular and well-known song from the record was "Lightworks," which sampled a track by the same name made in the 1960s by composer, bandleader, pianist, and inventor Raymond Scott (born Harry Warnow, 1908–1994). "Lightworks" was originally a jingle for a commercial back at a time where electronic music wasn't a genre. It was used for special effects and to produce commercial jingles to sell products.

"'Lightworks' was a jingle for a line of cosmetics," explains historian, producer, and archivist Jeff Winner. "And so what the lyrics are dealing with is talking about eye shadow and lipstick and stuff like that. And how these products are going to charm the pants off your man and make him buy you a ring. So, naturally, that's like a compelling, funny thing to listen to in modern times."

(opposite) Raymond Scott's Electronium (circa 1970) that he sold to Motown Records. Photos courtesy of Irwin Chusid.

 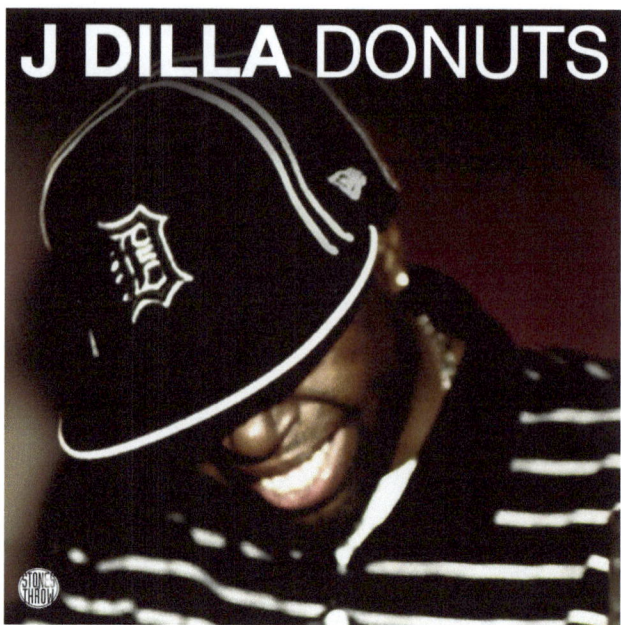

Dilla cleverly cut up and manipulated vocal clips "light up the skies" and "his heart does flips" to sound as though the singer was saying "Light up the spliffs," a marijuana culture reference. Raymond Scott was nerdy and square. He didn't socialize. He didn't party or get drunk. We're talking about someone who, according to his first wife, Pearl (via an interview with their son, Stan Warnow, for his documentary *Deconstructing Dad*), left his own wedding reception because he didn't want to be around so many people. And yet through Dilla's subtle, yet creative changes, Raymond Scott became synonymous with a culture and lifestyle he knew virtually nothing about. Dilla took the cosmetics jingle and turned it into a hip-hop song. "Dilla had lupus and was working on the album [*Donuts*], and the perfect storm of all of that is his final masterpiece," Jeff Winner muses. "He dies at a young age, tragically. Everyone loved the album. 'Lightworks' has become the track that most people reference and remember from that album. Or from Jay Dee in general.

"But he didn't really have to do much to it," Winner continues. "He took the entire track as it already existed [and] added like a different kind of percussive element. He also added a siren." Another crazy component to all this is that when *Donuts* was released in 2006, "Lightworks" was already half a century old. And yet it sounded like it could have been made yesterday. The music Raymond Scott was making in the 1950s and 1960s was so ahead of its time that it still appeals to artists and fans today. "That must have been what appealed to Dilla about it," Winner marvels.

Because of Dilla's slight manipulation of "Lightworks," the hip-hop community and fans were turned on to Raymond Scott. "His work with commercials always fascinated me since I was an advertising major," says Philadelphia DJ/producer King Britt. "Lightworks" would later be sampled by MF DOOM, and there are remixes that feature Q-Tip and Busta Rhymes.

No one even knew "Lightworks" existed until 2000 when Jeff Winner and Gert-Jan Blom produced *Manhattan Research Inc.*, a two-CD compilation of electronic music created by Raymond Scott. Without this release, Dilla would have never heard the song. *Manhattan Research Inc.* is still revered by many artists today. "Have you heard his *Manhattan [Research]* project?" Los Angeles producer Daedelus asks over coffee in Silver Lake. "Like that weird demo stuff he did for commercials was never meant to be used…but [it has] such a weird irreverent sense of humor that you find in hip-hop, directly. People loved 'Lightworks.' They loved that track by Dilla," Daedelus says. "It's one of his more kind of infamous tracks on its own. It's not one of his productions. It's really like a testament to Dilla and his invention. But then when you hear the original, it's like he didn't flip it super hard. He found it and he transformed it with his touch."

"I first heard about him when we got busted for a sample," Eothen Alapatt aka Egon recollects. "I was running Stones Throw at the time, and Irwin [Chusid], who is basically the administrator for the Raymond Scott estate, hit up Stones Throw shortly after Dilla's *Donuts* and explained that the album sampled one of Raymond Scott's compositions." The conversation with Irwin, combined with Alapatt's love for the song "Lightworks," piqued his curiosity, and he decided to look into Raymond Scott further. "The first person I hit up

(*top left*) Raymond Scott sits pensive in the studio. (*top right*) Scott at Three Willow Park, Long Island, New York, 1967. Photo by Jim Henson, courtesy of Irwin Chusid.
(*above*) Scott in front of his gear in his workshop in North Hills, New York, 1959.

was Madlib," Alapatt reminisces. "And I said, 'Do you know anything about this?' He's like, 'Oh yeah. I gave Dilla that record. Here's the record.' And he showed me the *Manhattan Research* record. I started listening to it, and I'm like, 'Oh, man, some of this stuff sounds so familiar.'"

"It's no small wonder that Madlib and Dilla were so intrigued by Raymond Scott," Alapatt continues. "Rhythmically, I think that he was working with ideas that made it very easy to use in a hip-hop context. Dilla used every aspect of Raymond Scott. He used drums from one track. He used 'The Tomorrow People' for the intro. And then he used that one 'Lightworks' thing."

In addition to "Lightworks," Dilla also sampled Raymond Scott's music on beat tapes that were never released. Same with Madlib. Madlib sampled Raymond's "Baltimore Gas & Electric Company" and "Ripples" for "Electric Company (Voltage-Watts)," a track from Stones Throw's *Beat Konducta: Movie Scenes*. "That's one of the ones that came out that Irwin busted us for," Egon explains. "And when I say 'busted us for,' I mean it in the nicest sort of way. He wasn't a dick about it."

At the time that Raymond Scott was making this crazy, quirky electronic music, no one was really interested. As far as his experimental electronic music, "No one really seemed to pay attention to [Raymond Scott] or what he was doing," Jeff Winner elucidates. "All this stuff has been recent." Dilla wasn't the first artist to sample from *Manhattan Research*. The Gorillaz did in 2001. They had a song on their first album called "Man Research," a play on *Manhattan Research*. At the time, they didn't realize they were headed for a huge career, so they just didn't even bother clearing the sample. "They surprised themselves by selling so many copies of the album," Winner explains. "They set a *Guinness Book* world record for sales by a virtual group on their first album for copies sold."

But even with the Gorillaz sampling Raymond Scott's music first, it wasn't until 2006, when Dilla's *Donuts* was released, that hip-hop fans, and even artists, found out about him. Scott was a household name during the 1930s, '40s, and '50s for working as a bandleader for various, more traditional entities, such as his own Quintette, the CBS radio network, and the popular radio/TV show *Your Hit Parade* (first on CBS radio then on to NBC for TV); however, it was "Dilla's use of 'Lightworks' that raised the profile of obviously the track itself and Raymond in general," Winner says. "And it has brought a lot of people to investigate him and what he did. That track would never have been…it was not even like a track. I don't even know how to explain this to you, but it was never put on a record during Raymond Scott's lifetime."

(*above right*) Raymond Scott at Three Willow Park during a 1967 recording session for a Bufferin commercial. Photo by Jim Henson, courtesy of Irwin Chusid.

While Raymond Scott is probably known to most of today's music fans for "Lightworks" and Dilla, he was also the man behind songs heard on *Looney Tunes* and *Merrie Melodies* cartoons. When Scott composed songs such as "The Penguin" and "Powerhouse," he didn't intend for them to be used for cartoons. They were pop songs. But Warner Bros. music director Carl Stalling loved the quirkiness of these songs and thought they would be perfect for his shows.

There are various layers and facets of Raymond Scott's career. In addition to his clever and quirky music, he was also an inventor, creating many innovative instruments and machines. "After *Your Hit Parade* went off the air in 1957, '58, Raymond pretty much went into his man cave or his laboratory and wanted to create. He wanted to be an engineer. He no longer wanted to be a musician or a bandleader dealing with live musicians," explains music historian, biographer, and Raymond Scott estate administrator Irwin Chusid.

One of Scott's inventions was the Electronium, an idea-generating and music-composing device. In 1970, Motown founder Berry Gordy read a *Variety* magazine article about the Electronium. Fascinated by Scott's creative vision, Gordy visited Scott at Three Willow Park in Long Island to hear and see a demonstration. Gordy was so impressed that he offered Scott $10,000 to build an Electronium for Motown. Scott agreed, and he and his then wife Mitzi moved to L.A.

In a 1982 interview, Scott told music teacher, historian, and lecturer Tom Rhea that the Electronium was a "guided missile" that he guided by pressing buttons. Hoby Cook, an engineer at Motown, described the device as a "masterpiece of intuitive thought." Motown artists such as Michael Jackson were also impressed with the innovative device.

"The Electronium was a cabinet with its control panel intact, but the only thing that worked is, if you plugged it in, it would light up, 'cause Raymond had cannibalized the circuitry for other projects," Irwin Chusid explains. "And there's still a lot of interest in trying to restore the Electronium, and it's problematic. Nobody's quite sure how it works. The Electronium was never finished." A restoration attempt is currently being made in Los Angeles by Brian Kehew, a keyboard tech for the Who.

The Electronium was so innovative and ahead of its time that it continues to amaze and inspire artists of all different genres over twenty years after his death. One such artist is Ahmir "Questlove" Thompson. In 2013, Thompson hosted Electronium: The Future Was Then, a two-night event in Brooklyn that celebrated early electronic music pioneers such as Raymond Scott and Robert Moog, the inventor of the Moog synthesizer. In an interview with Ben Greenman, Questlove explained that Raymond Scott doesn't really get the credit he deserves, as most people think of Robert Moog as "the father" of electronic music. "This machine [the Electronium] was basically kinda the idea of the first use of 'modern sound' in music," Questlove elucidated to Greenman.

"The electronic stuff is pretty interesting," Irwin Chusid says of Raymond Scott's music. "Electronic music nowadays is kinda sleek. Kinda shiny. Kinda sparkly. Kinda metallic. It's kinda synthetic, it's kinda fake. But you know, a lot you can do with it. Not to put down electronic music, but Raymond put an analog warmth [into it]."

Raymond Scott was one of the only musicians in history to be productive in both the big band and electronic music eras. "There's only one other person I can think of," Chusid muses, "Sun Ra. I can't think of anyone else." They both grew up on big bands and eventually each had their own. And later in their careers, they were able to successfully transition into the electronic music world.

"I hate electronic music, because human beings are quivering organisms," Scott once said of his music. "My designs, although electronic, always quiver." Raymond Scott was quiet, reserved, and generally pretty secretive about his inventions, but it's still not entirely clear why he hasn't received the respect and fame he deserves. Had it not been for Dilla's *Donuts*, many hip-hop fans and even artists may have never known the name Raymond Scott. Dilla, an innovator in his own right, sat on his hospital bed and through a slight manipulation was able to turn a quirky cosmetics jingle into one of the most revered hip-hop songs of our generation.

"I mean, I don't know. It's one of those things where he's really fundamental to me," Daedelus says. "Before 'Lightworks,' I didn't know if people understood."

To this day, Daedelus still wows crowds when he DJs Raymond Scott's music. "I still blow minds when I DJ some of his stuff," Daedelus says. "Like 'The Bass-Line Generator,' that song from *Manhattan Research*. It speaks so much to an aesthetic of minimalism and direct communication of a simple melody. Which was so prevalent in music now. And so when you play it for somebody, and they're like, 'When is this from?' And you give them the details and they freak out, and it's reasonable. So it's still blowing minds."

"Certainly, Raymond Scott would not have predicted [hip-hop's embrace of his music] or understood it, really," Jeff Winner muses. And Winner couldn't have predicted it either. "Like when me and my colleague [Gert-Jan Blom] who coproduced that compilation with me—we didn't even fully realize what was about to happen," he reminisces. "We just loved the material. We didn't necessarily realize that everyone else was going to also." ○

(opposite) "A Cockpit of Dreams." Photo by David Garh, courtesy of Irwin Chusid.

Susaye Greene got her first gig at eighteen months old, acting in a baby food commercial. As a teenager, she went on tour with Harry Belafonte. She joined Ray Charles's Raelettts in the late '60s, then went on to sing and write with Stevie Wonder, collaborating most memorably on "I Can't Help It," which Michael Jackson recorded for 1979's *Off the Wall*. After leaving Wonder, Greene joined the Supremes in their final incarnation.

Ray of Light

interview by Travis Atria with intro by Brian DiGenti

"You see, being a Supreme is very important to me," singer-songwriter Susaye Greene told *Blues & Soul* at the end of 1976, just after the release of her second Supremes album, *Mary, Scherrie & Susaye*. "And since I believe show business is a question of steps and sections, I attach equal importance to every era I undertake."

"I actually started out with Harry Belafonte," she explained, "but the time I spent with Ray Charles was the first period of learning really for me. Without that experience, and the time that I later spent with Stevie, I don't think I could have been ready for this period in my career."

Greene was excited about the future, about writing new material. "I've become more involved with writing this year than I have ever been—even than when I was with Stevie Wonder and Wonderland," she mused at the time. "After spending a year and a half with Stevie, the talent has to rub off on you, and I guess I must have a hundred of my songs completed now and I plan to publish them all…and distribute them to people that I feel would be best suited," she said. "Certainly, some of them will be earmarked for the Supremes!"

That was the plan anyway. But original Supreme Mary Wilson put the kibosh on having Greene and Scherrie Payne write songs for the next Supremes album, and the group subsequently disbanded forever. While the move stung at the time, it brought about Susaye Greene's best album, the 1979 quiet storm/modern-soul classic from the former Supremes duo Scherrie and Susaye, *Partners*, produced by Eugene McDaniels.

Wax Poetics spoke to Greene about her journey.

(opposite) Promotional photo of Susaye Greene.

When did you start singing with Ray Charles?

I guess, it would be around 1968. I had been in Los Angeles with my mom [Vivian Greene], and she had a friend named Dee Irwin, who had a song that went [*sings*] "Would you like to swing on a star?" ["Swinging on a Star"] was a pretty big hit for him. At any rate, Dee was handling Ray's publishing company at the time. When my mom called him, he said Ray was looking for a new singer. That's how it started. I went up to his studio, Ray asked if I had a particular song, and I sang a song called "Unchained Melody." He asked if I knew any standards, and I sang "My Funny Valentine," which had always been a bit of a showstopper for me as well. I knew the key it was in, and he played for me. Eventually, that was one of the solos I had in the show. I was hired to sing solos and sing with the Raeletts as well. Because I'm very quick with parts, my job was to know everybody's parts, which I'm sure got on everybody's nerves because I was younger. But I was trained. Music has been my life. Consequently, I went to work for him that evening.

Wow, that same night?

Yeah, the same thing happened with Stevie Wonder, but that's another story.

We'll get to that one.

So, Ray had a gig at the Cocoanut Grove, a very illustrious nightclub in L.A. I remember Barbra Streisand was there in the audience and Jesse Jackson. A lot of very famous people. Ray was so popular as a person, not just as a star or an artist. He was a very popular person. He loved people, even though he loved his privacy. He was tremendous fun.

So, you joined Ray in the late '60s. If I have the time line correct, he had recently gone through trouble with the law and gotten clean from heroin.

Yes.

Also, at that point, he'd been on top of the music world for so long. Was his career on a downslide?

Without any success or any money coming in, he would have been doing this [anyway]. He would have been in some bar playing music. The money was just cream, as they say. But at this time, he'd been through rehab. He said he didn't really have any dreams left. And because I am who I am, I was the right person for him to say that to, I think, because I had so much enthusiasm and optimism. [*shouts*] "No dreams? How can you say that?" I played Jimi Hendrix for Ray, and people he'd never had the time to listen to. He was a workaholic. He was on the road all the time. He didn't like going out all the time, because once you're out, then you're Ray Charles. We went more places than I think he'd been in years. I'd say, "You gotta see Gladys [Knight] and the Pips," you know? I know that he was by that time greatly jaded to the world and the ways of the business. He was still recording. He was always going to record, whether they were extremely successful or not. When you are famous like Ray, the strange part is, how visible you are and yet how to maintain your privacy. He was a blind man who could get in a taxi and go anywhere in the world, and did, on his own. Because everybody in the world knows him. I don't care where you are. If you go to Africa or Afghanistan, they all know Ray Charles.

You mentioned introducing him to Hendrix and all these new things. What did he think of it?

He was always very straightforward. No airs, no graces. Straight from the hip. I played him—I believe it was *Band of Gypsys*, because I was crazy about that album. He said, "I understand it," but it wasn't his bag. When he would listen to music, he'd listen to gospel. He carried his own reel-to-reel tape recorder around, and he had bags of tapes. He'd play Billie Holiday, when she was a kid. I mean, she was maybe fifteen or sixteen. I don't know where he got these tapes from, but somebody's always giving you something when you're admired on that scale.

I spoke several years ago to Bobby Womack, who played guitar with Ray. He said the audition process was very nerve-racking, that Ray was kind of a taskmaster. Did you find him that way?

Not *kind of*. [*laughs*] He *was*. He was a consummate musician, you see. He used to say, "I can hear a rat pee on cotton." He was very succinct, very astute, and as far as the music goes, he was depending on his ears, so he had to be a step ahead. He had written most of the arrangements, so he knew what they were in his head, and he was very much like this: If he saw you were a great musician, then he would respect your musicianship and give you your freedom to do what you do best. But if you were messing up, especially onstage, he would let you know. Right then. Onstage. He would say your name, and then he would tell you what you were doing wrong. You didn't want to be in that crowd.

I can imagine.

I was just a kid surrounded by [Ray's] eighteen-piece band. Henry Coker on trombone and Fathead Newman on saxophone. Lord have mercy, these were some of the greatest

(*opposite*) Ray Charles and the Raeletts during *The Carol Burnett Show* in 1972. (left to right) Vernita Moss, Dorothy Berry, Mable John, Susaye Greene, and Estella Yarbrough.

musicians ever. I was there during several configurations of the big band. It was a place of respect. You were a professional, and you were expected to behave as a professional. I have to say, he never had to call my name. Even as a kid, this was my milieu. I knew what I was doing.

You say you got the job that first night. What was it like? Did you go on the road immediately?

Yes. I can remember the first three gigs we did out of town. We were at the Cocoanut Grove here in L.A.; we rehearsed all day long. I had to learn all of the backgrounds. He knew he could depend on me to sing a solo. We went next to San Francisco. I was onstage rehearsing "My Funny Valentine," and Duke Ellington came in.

Wow.

Exactly. That's how everyone was, especially me. He stayed for the rehearsal. Afterward, Ray introduced me to him and he said, "Kid, you've got pipes." I'll never forget it.

That's a pretty good endorsement.

There you go. But we stayed so many places, we traveled so many places. We were on the road nine months out of the year. We traveled on buses a lot. Ray had his own wonderful bus. We traveled on his plane. He had a small Cessna as well as a big jet that carried the band. There was a private section in the back, a kitchen and galley. It was a tremendous experience traveling with Ray. He would play chess with his valet. He was ruthless! And he'd talk trash. He'd say, "Well, you got eyes." He'd play chess with Dizzy Gillespie, just so many iconic, classic musicians.

Was he close with the band, or was he more removed from you?

I wouldn't say he was removed. As I said, he was a very private person. He had a lazy attitude about him in that he could just *chill*. But he was a tremendously responsible person. He knew he was the boss. He knew he had to set an example. He expected you to be on time. He'd charge you fifty dollars if you were one second late. It taught you to be really on it and to be a professional. To always be *on* for your performances. I stood backstage every night. We'd get dressed, and I'd hurry so I could watch his part before the Raeletts came on, because it was an education in brilliance, it was a musical education, an education in performance, and in reading your audience.

(*opposite*) The Raeletts promotional photo from Tangerine Records, circa 1975. (left to right) Vernita Moss, Susaye Greene, and Mable John, with another Raelett. Photo courtesy of Susaye Greene.

How did the shows work, then? He'd go out by himself first?

The band would start. Leroy Cooper, who was the bandleader—they called him the Burgermeister; he weighed about three hundred fifty—he played a big baritone sax, and he'd come in the dressing room and they'd discuss what the lineup for the night was. Ray would give him the tempos, and you had to anticipate where it was going. Ray was a fierce, fierce person. He had this energy just pop off of him. He liked to have his drink before the show. He drank, I mean, it was no secret, he drank Bols Genever gin. It was like white lightning. You'd open the bottle and your head would be swimming. He drank it in his coffee with lots of sugar, and by the time he was ready to go onstage, he was just rocking and smiling and laughing. He was so passionate about music. He said, "I'd do it for free, but don't tell anybody."

So you went pretty much from Ray right to Stevie Wonder, is that right?

There were a few events in the middle. I sang with the New Birth. Harvey Fuqua was a friend, so when he started his company and was producing for RCA, the New Birth had some difficulty with the young lady who was in the group, so I sang, "Until It's Time for You to Go." That was their first million-seller. I didn't get credit for that for years and years, until the Internet.

It's interesting you'd end up with Stevie Wonder after Ray, because they seem so connected. Apart from the fact they're both blind piano players; musically, Stevie seems so influenced by Ray Charles. How did you get involved with him?

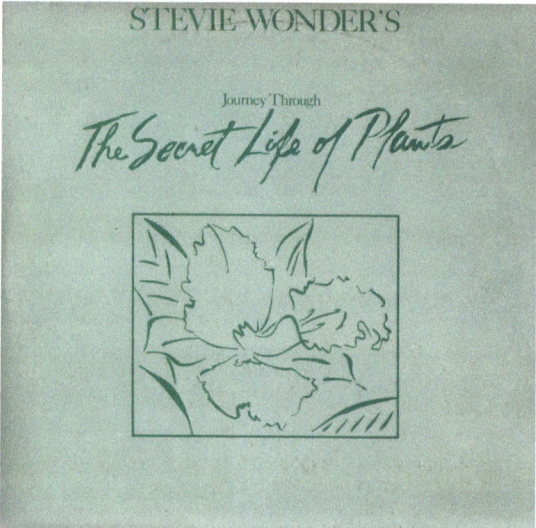

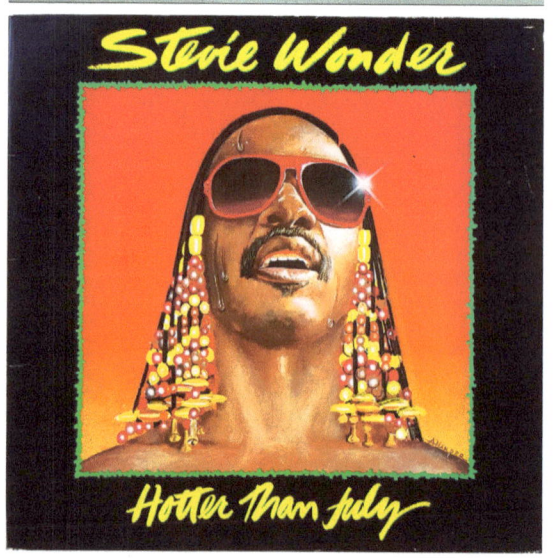

(*top left*) Susaye Greene and songwriting partner Stevie Wonder.
Photo courtesy of Susaye Greene.

Well, here we go again. My mom was so influential in my life. She was on the board of the NAACP in Beverly Hills. On this board was Bob Jones, who became [Michael] Jackson's publicity liaison. It just came to me. I wanted to see if I could write with Stevie Wonder. Bob said, "Call the office." Calvin, who is Stevie's oldest brother, answered the phone. He said, "Steve's looking for somebody right now. Why don't you come on down and sing for him?" It was a hotel in Hollywood on Sunset. His whole band stayed there. They were rehearsing, and everybody was still waiting for Steve to arrive. Stevie Wonder is always late, which is so ironic, because I told you about the fifty dollars you'd lose with Ray if you were one second late. That continued. I'd show up for rehearsal, there would be no one there. Four hours later, I'd call, "Where is everyone?" They'd say, "Is he there?" It took me a while to get it.

Quite a different experience.

Like chalk and cheese. It was a rock-and-roll life. That was the main difference between working with Steve and working with Ray. Ray was this independent person who would get in a cab and go to Paris. Steve, wherever he is right now, he's surrounded by at least ten people. He's not going anywhere without that crowd. Ray played theaters. Steve plays arenas. That was some of the most exciting times I've had in my life. All you had to do was sit and watch, and it was like, "Here comes Yoko Ono." Like that.

Tell me about writing with him. I know you did "I Can't Help It" for Michael Jackson.

Steve and I are almost psychic with each other. He can tell you. He'll start a sentence and I can finish it. We started writing immediately. It was just, "That's why I'm here." He's a big kid. That's who he is. He's enthusiastic. He's extremely enthusiastic about his music, and it flows. I've never met anyone that writes like that. I would basically get a tape recorder and just follow him around. He'd yell, "Sue! Get this one!" He'd sing and these melodies would pour out of him [*scats*], you know, no words. And for some reason, when I hear these sounds he makes, I know what he's trying to say.

Did you write lyrics and he'd do the music?

It was very free-form and it depends on the song. "I Can't Help It," he had most of the melody. He had the hooks, and you say, "No, don't do that, go *up*."

You were with him at an unprecedented peak in his career. I know you sang on "Joy Inside My Tears."

That was a very emotional time for him. He had been through a terrible accident [in 1973]. His driver had fallen asleep at the wheel, and there was a truck in front of him that had long boards hanging out the back, and they just barreled into it. He was asleep. If he had been awake, it would have cut his head off. He still has a terrible scar. He almost died. When I met him, he was recuperating, and he hadn't been back to work in a while. He was itching to go. He was in love, but he was always in love. None of my business.

Was that around the early '70s?

It must have been 1974. Just before I joined the Supremes. He was having some difficulties. This is how "Joy Inside My Tears" came about. He had recorded the track, and I could tell he was very sad. He was being pressured. He was always being pressured by women. He was sad and he didn't know what to do. We were always friends, and I said to him, "You shouldn't really marry. If you want to have the kids, just pay for them." It's much easier than going through relationships, and I've always been honest to my men friends particularly who are in show business. What you want is the joy, so just present that. Women will take it. "Here's money, go away." They'll call it what they call it, but it's much more real than going through relationships that don't last, being unhappy, making people have expectations, and all of that. That song came out of that talk. It was quite a dramatic moment in his life.

So that song is about you?

Not about me.

I mean, about that conversation?

Sure, sure. There is a song that's about me, but I'm not going to tell you which one it is.

No! I'll just have to go listen closely.

That's how it is. [*laughs*]

In *20 Feet From Stardom*, the 2013 film about backup singers, it's clear that you have an interesting perspective on fame. You've been around it your whole life but have managed to keep a somewhat normal personal life. That must have been hard to keep up when you joined the Supremes and were front and center.

The thing is, Travis, I was groomed for show business. I had my first job at eighteen months.

That's right, a baby food commercial.

Sure. By the time I was twelve, I had my union card. I went to professional children's school. All the kids were pros. It was such a rarefied atmosphere. You got little kids walking around talking about their agents. The Supremes happened because, once again, who comes up? My mother. Bob Jones told her Cindy Birdsong was leaving and they were looking for a way to revamp the Supremes. They had been under contract for three years but hadn't recorded anything. I met with Pedro Ferrer, who was Mary Wilson's husband and the manager of the group. He explained Cindy was leaving and they needed someone who could write for the group.

By this time [in 1976], "Free" had become a hit. That was Deniece Williams's first million-seller that I cowrote with her and Hank Redd and Nate Watts. It had become number one in England. Well, timing being everything, I met with Mary. It was a very difficult situation because she handled the business and her husband was the manager. I was signed to write for the Supremes and add my style to the group. Mary didn't really want there to be another lead singer, but we recorded "High Energy," and it was my lead, and it became a dance hit for the Supremes.

I was greatly disappointed when Mary told me she didn't want me to write for the group anymore. It was what made it worthwhile to me. I came from a place where I had my freedom. When I was with Wonderlove, I got to sing what I wanted to sing. We opened the show. That's primarily what we did in Wonderlove, is write. We wrote so many songs together. When I joined, Stevie wasn't on the road, but he was paying us to rehearse six days a week.

So, push forward and I'm standing in Mary Wilson's fabulous bedroom, and she said, "Well, I don't think we're ready for one of the Supremes to be a writer." There would have been a control thing. She had been through so much with all the configurations, and it was Mary's life, the Supremes. I remember Cindy told me when [Diana Ross] left, after the show in Vegas, Mary got hysterical. She thought it was over. It was very difficult for her. We could have gone on forever, but Pedro encouraged Mary to leave the group because he couldn't control the group. It was a sad time.

It sounds like a tough situation.

It really was. Mary left and we began looking for someone to go into the group, at which time Mary and Diana Ross went to Berry Gordy and said, "If there's no original Supreme in the group, it should end." And that's what happened. ⬤

(*opposite*) The Last Supremes. (left to right) Susaye Greene, Mary Wilson, and Scherrie Payne. Photo by David Redfern/Getty Images.

R&B Avant-Garde

P.M. Dawn broke musical boundaries people hadn't even yet considered. Prince Be was ahead of his time, pioneering singing and rapping within a modern R&B mode. At the time, the group was misunderstood, underappreciated, or just plain hated on. But now it's clear in today's hip-hop and R&B landscape, Prince Be is the father of the style.

by Michael A. Gonzales

"If P.M. Dawn came out today they would be Gods," someone recently posted on Twitter, and, as a fan of the group's avant-garde hip-hop soul sound since the beginning of their careers, I can't help but agree. Certainly, unlike the closed minds of decades past that had a problem with the cosmic freakiness of Prince Be (Attrell Cordes) and his one-year-younger brother DJ Minutemix (Jarrett Cordes) introduced in 1991, new-millennium fans are more open towards experimentation. In addition, artists such as Kanye West and Childish Gambino—who once covered the duo's wondrous soul track "I'd Die Without You"—have celebrated P.M. Dawn's innovation and taken it as inspiration

These days, we can hear and see P.M. Dawn's influence in artists such as Solange, Frank Ocean, and other kooky creatives who have no problem waving their freak flags in stereo. Certainly, as *Record Redux* book series author and Albumism columnist Quentin Harrison says, "P.M. Dawn's sound and visual aesthetics always felt like the 'something from another time' and that 'against the grain' motif they wielded fearlessly has been taken up en masse by others. At the same time (in the 1990s), acts like Maxwell, Erykah Badu, and D'Angelo (among others) were reaping the benefits of the path P.M. Dawn helped pave for neo-soul."

Back in the day, things weren't always so diverse. As someone who lived through the gritty boom-bap era of the 1990s' realness when roughness equaled righteousness, rap music could be a brutal, sometimes deadly, profession, and the slightest dis could lead to the coldest response either on record or in person. In the case of P.M. Dawn's clash with self-proclaimed teacher KRS-One in 1992, it was unexpected. "I never knew there was a beef until that night," Prince Be told me in 1995 when I interviewed him for *Vibe* magazine. Be was flopped down onto a comfortable white leather sofa in the living room of his Jersey City penthouse. A signed lithograph self-portrait of John Lennon hung over a table. "Even when we saw him that night, we were like, 'Oh shit, there goes KRS-One.' We were excited, but he just looked at us like we were insane."

It was an MTV-sponsored event at New York's Sound Factory nightclub. The eclectic duo was already onstage and had performed one song. The year before, they released their groundbreaking debut, *Of the Heart, of the Soul and of the Cross: The Utopian Experience*, an album recorded in England, where the brothers had relocated after signing with Gee Street Records in 1989. *New York Daily News* music columnist Jim Farber defined *Of the Heart…* as "a kind of soft revolution, critiquing the world by refusing any involvement. Instead they've proposed a kind of defiant hedonism, a purposeful apathy. For rap that's a first: expressing rebellion through escape rather than anger."

However, that night at the Sound Factory, there was anger in the air. Just as P.M. Dawn was about to do their mega-hit, "Set Adrift on Memory Bliss," a track that sampled Spandau Ballet's 1983 New Romantic plastic-soul ballad "True," things quickly went askew. While the song was P.M. Dawn's second single, with the first being the trippy bounce of "A Watcher's Point of View (Don't 'Cha Think)," it was "Set Adrift on Memory Bliss" that became a major crossover smash and the first Black rap single to reach number one on the pop charts. Still, P.M. Dawn's pop/MTV success did little to endear them the hard-core hip-hop gatekeepers.

While the perceived softness of P.M. Dawn's music and Afro-psychedelic personas (Lennonesque shades, hippy beads, cloud-covered clothing) already made them suspect, it didn't help that months before their Sound Factory appearance, in the pages of *Details* magazine, Be questioned KRS-One's scholarly credentials ("KRS-One wants to be a teacher, but a teacher of what?"), which gave the rapper, along with his Boogie Down Productions posse, carte blanche to crash the duo's set. He and his brother Kenny stormed P.M. Dawn's set, and KRS-One shoved Prince Be off the stage. Meanwhile, Kenny jacked the turntables and started spinning the BDP battle cry "The Bridge Is Over."

Recording engineer and producer Scott Harding (aka Scotty Hard), who worked with the Cordes brothers at Calliope Studios, where he engineered the demo recording of "Reality Used to Be a Friend of Mine," was at that show. Years later, he is still disgusted by what he witnessed. "Prince Be was a big guy, but he was like a teddy bear, so KRS-One found no resistance there," Harding recalls. "It was a real invasion, and Prince Be didn't deserve that. But P.M. Dawn was blowing up, they had a pop hit, and people resented that."

Former Rush Management publicist Bill Adler, who had previously worked with alternative hip-hop/Native Tongue rappers De La Soul, was the Island Records press agent in 1992 and worked with P.M. Dawn on their first project. "When De La put out 'Me, Myself and I,' they clowned the limitations and aggressiveness of acts like Run-DMC," Alder says. "But, Run-DMC merely brushed it off, while KRS-One lost his mind. But he has always had a dual identity between having good politics and being a thug. I wasn't at the show, but the next day the office was crazy, and it generated a bunch of press. But it puzzled me why so many people were taking KRS's side."

As though the beatdown wasn't enough, bad luck hit early in Be's career, as Anil Dash reported in his stunning 2016 article "Set Adrift: Beneath the Surface of P.M. Dawn": "Later that same year, Prince Be entered a three-day coma right in the midst of their biggest run of hit songs. He was diagnosed with diabetes, and its complications would dog him for the rest of his life."

Twenty-six years later, younger brother Jarrett Cordes says from his home in New Jersey, "When all of that KRS-One stuff happened, it had a real effect on my brother. KRS could've pulled my brother to the side and talked to him, or anything else besides a physical altercation. Afterwards, Be even started calling himself the Nocturnal, because, he claimed it was a way to balance his positivity and negativity. All of that KRS stuff brought out a darkness in him that you can hear on tracks he made later that year like 'The Nocturnal Is in the House' and 'Plastic.'"

Both songs were featured on P.M. Dawn's sophomore 1993 release, *The Bliss Album…?* In an interview with *Melody Maker* that same year, Prince Be explained, "It's like a documentary of what happened to me since the last album. I'm looking for the reasons for everything. I'd like an answer. To what, I have no idea. But I came up with no answers, no reasons. It's called *The Bliss Album* sarcastically. The music is very out and laid back, but at times it gets to be real angry."

Decades later, the KRS-One attack often seems to be more celebrated than the innovative music Prince Be left behind when he passed away on June 17, 2016, at the age of forty-six. Jarrett sang the P.M. Dawn soul hit "I'll Die Without You" at Be's homegoing services, shocking many in the church who didn't realize that he had the chops. "Be and I sang together on many of those songs," he says. "People just assumed that it was just him."

Be's underappreciated aural legacy can be heard in P.M. Dawn's four (commercially released) albums, with *Jesus Wept* being my personal favorite, as well as their remixes and outside productions for acts that included Elton John ("When I Think About Love"), Philip Bailey ("I Won't Open My Arms"), George Michael ("Killer/Papa Was a Rollin' Stone"), Cathy Dennis ("Falling"), Ambersunshower ("Running Song"), and a little-known rap group, Moodswingaz, that featured by Be's baby bro Jason.

Journalist Jon Caramanica noted in Be's *New York Times* obituary, "Even in an era of earnest bohemianism in hip-hop, P.M. Dawn stood out for its hippie-esque mysticism, fantastical imagery, crypto-Christian references and ethereal musical aesthetic. Prince Be was an early blurrer of the lines between rapping and singing, and between the earthly and the spiritual...."

When he was healthy, Prince Be was like mountain with feet. Standing six feet four inches tall, he was a giant of a man with the talent to match. A welcoming collaborator in every aspect of P.M. Dawn's albums and singles, he worked closely with everyone from the musicians to the engineers to the graphic designers. "I thought of P.M. Dawn as De La Soul meets the Beach Boys," says writer Amy Linden. "Production-wise, Prince Be was like Brian Wilson, but without the mental illness and drugs."

Still, while Be was the chief auteur behind their sound, he and Jarrett collaborated closely when it came to choosing samples. "A sample can make or break a song," Jarrett says. According to the younger Cordes brother, it was his idea to use elements of the Gil Scott-Heron track "Angola, Louisiana" to construct "Paper Doll," and he also suggested the drums from the Soul Searchers' "Ashley's Roachclip" for "Set Adrift..." Jarrett laughs at the memory. "We always fought over samples, and with the planning of each album, we would break up. [Gee Street founder/president] Jon Baker used to call and ask if we had finished fighting. He'd say, 'Can y'all brothers get your shit out so we can actually get some work done.' He did that with every project."

According to engineer Michael Fossenkemper, who worked closely with P.M. Dawn for years, "Be relied on Jarrett to get stuff on tape and to be another set of ears. Jarrett was instrumental, and Be needed to have him around. I don't think he could function without Jarrett around." In 1995, Be explained to me, "I think the songs should be interpretations of the emotions, so we make the music first, and whatever the music brings out is what the lyrics are about. I'm like a kite, and Jarrett keeps me from going too far out there. If I go way out there, I will either fall or keep going."

In fact, no matter how much they might've argued about loops and beats, once the smoke cleared, they realized that they were blessed to be doing exactly what they always dreamt when they were just MTV-watching boys. "We were just two kids from Lincoln Park, New Jersey, who came from nothing and literally made our way to be part of musical history," Jarrett says. "We were brothers, so we fought and went through our stupid brother shit, but we also had number one records and got to work with our heroes. When we left Jersey for England, all we had was guts and a dream. I think that says a lot."

In the beginning, there was MTV. Launched in 1981 when the Cordes brothers weren't yet teenagers, the twenty-four-hour video channel started the ball rolling on the "second British Invasion" that introduced them to Culture Club, Duran Duran, the Human League, the Police, Depeche Mode, and Spandau Ballet. "When we became conscious of music, it was the '80s," Prince Be said a few months before the release of their third album, *Jesus Wept*, which critic Jim DeRogatis has called "a psychedelic masterpiece."

"I was an '80s kid listening to Michael Jackson, George Michael, Prince, and Cyndi Lauper," Be said, "but we were from an urban area and there was hip-hop everywhere. Some of the biggest innovations in music were coming out of hip-hop, and we were witnesses to that." Still, as much as they liked the new pop and hip-hop of the '80s, Prince Be was always digging deeper and discovering the dusty sounds of Jimi Hendrix, the Beatles, Harry Nilsson, Joni Mitchell, Sly Stone, Paul Williams, Brian Wilson, and Phil Spector.

"To me, my brother was Brian Spector," Jarrett jokes. "He experimented a lot, because he never wanted P.M. Dawn to sound too normal." A few years before our meeting, Island Records (Gee Street's parent company) publicist Bill Adler gave me an advance of P.M. Dawn's breathtaking debut. I assumed they were British and was surprised to learn that they hailed from New Jersey from right across the Hudson.

"My mom had six boys, so she worked a lot," Jarrett says. "Somebody had to cook and clean, and that was me. Be would help them with their homework, and us being responsible for the kids made our bond that much closer. We started our first group with my uncle Tim, who called himself Courageous Cuts; I was Minutemix [an homage to Bob Kane's cartoon TV show *Courageous Cat and Minute Mouse*]; and there was Prince Be. My uncle was in it just to have fun, but as Be and I got more serious, it became just the two of us."

During those years, the brothers performed at house parties where Be gained a rep for being an awesome MC and a crazy

"Cozmo D" Cenac, a founding member and producer behind electro rap group Newcleus whose "Jam On Revenge (The Wikki-Wikki Song)" was a hit in 1983.

"After a while, Al decided to sign them," Cozmo says from his home in Brooklyn, "but he needed someone to work with them in the studio, so that was my introduction to the group." McLaran and Cozmo were also partners in Pet Project Records, a subsidiary of Warlock, and the label P.M. Dawn was eventually signed to. Located in Cozmo's mother's basement in Park Slope, Brooklyn, his Transitions Studios was where they recorded "Ode to a Forgetful Mind (It's a Shame)," which was released in 1989. Cozmo remembers, "They were completely raw; they knew nothing yet. But Jarrett only came to the studio one time. It was just me and Be doing all the work."

Eleven years older, Cozmo adopted Be as his little brother. "He was only seventeen, but he was a big kid. At the same time, he was also very deep," says Cozmo. "We would talk for hours, having these metaphysical conversations. He was into the Native Tongues, and he wanted to meet those guys; but I told him, 'You have to up [politically], because those guys are conscious.' Be was the type of guy who would be conscious one minute and upsetting people the next. I tried to school him on the complexities of life, especially when it comes to the music business, but he wasn't trying to hear that. His philosophy was simple—he was just about peace, love, and making records."

The recording process went smoothly, though Cozmo does recall that when Prince Be told him he wanted to sing on the track, he laughed. "I said, 'Man, you can't sing.' He insisted that he could, but it didn't come out quite right. Later, I was shocked when they started releasing songs that were mostly singing. When I heard 'I'd Die Without You,' I was blown away, because I didn't know he had those kinds of chops. We didn't work long enough to get into an R&B side. Ours was strictly hip-hop, which he was dope as hell at doing. If he had decided to, Be could've been one of the all-time best rappers, because his skills were that good."

In the meantime, McLaran got Jarrett a mailroom job at Warlock where Prince Be also hung out on the regular. It was in the office where they befriended labelmate and future collaborator Todd Terry, a dance-music artist and remixer whose energetic track "I Love the Way You Shake" they would later sample for their hip-house track "Shake." Warlock/Pet Project released the 12-inch of "Ode to a Forgetful Mind (It's A Shame)," whose label only had Prince Be's name listed as the artist although Jarrett was credited as one of the producers alongside Be and Cozmo.

Unfortunately, Warlock did very little to promote the record. "Basically, they didn't push it at all," Cozmo says. However, U.K. partner Gee Street Records, who licensed the Warlock roster overseas, was having success with P.M. Dawn, getting their single radio spins and positive press. One

beatboxer. Jarrett says, "He would have beatbox battles and just slay people." It was during that time that the brothers decided to try to make records for real. "We actually sat down one day after school and talked about what we wanted to do with the rest of our lives. We were totally consumed by rap music, and decided to produce some tracks. Prince Be was reading a religious magazine called *The Plain Truth* and had seen the slogan that read, 'In the darkest hours comes the light.' Be said, 'That's phat. That's kind of like P.M. Dawn.' That's how we got our name."

Although the brothers were fans of everyone from Big Daddy Kane to future foe KRS-One, it was their love for the Jungle Brothers' 1988 album *Straight out the Jungle* that gave them the courage to submit their cassette demo to the group's label Warlock Records. "To this day, Uncle Tim is a garbage man, and he knew we were looking for different kinds of records to sample," Jarrett explains. "One day, he found this crate of records that someone had dumped in the trash. We listened to them and found this Ruby Andrews album, and found a sample on there that was just crazy.

"Back in those days, we didn't have anything to sample with, so we used a cassette deck. We would just record little pieces of what we needed, and paused it, then did it again until we had this three-minute piece of sample. We did all those early demos like that." The homemade tape found its way to the label's A&R man Al "T" McLaran, who was undecided on whether he should sign P.M. Dawn. Al called his homeboy Ben

afternoon when Gee Street president Jon Baker was visiting the Warlock office, he and Prince Be began talking about P.M. Dawn signing with his label. According to Jarrett, "Jon just told him straight, 'Listen, I'm on your record more than Warlock is. You guys are awesome, but Warlock is not doing shit for you. I would like you guys to sign with me.' Prince Be told me about their conversation and suggested we meet. Jon had already given him a [U.K.] magazine that was giving critical acclaim to 'Ode...' and it was obvious he was busting his ass."

Yet, somehow in the conversation, Pet Project Records owners McLaran and Cozmo were divided. "We were not moving any records, and Al wanted to sell their contract to Gee Street, but I was trying to start a new label called Black & Electric with P.M. Dawn as our star act," Cozmo says. "Next thing I knew, Be said they were going to England. I told them they couldn't go, because they were signed to me, but he just ignored me. We ended up with our lawyer signing over our rights to them. We got paid, but it was a bad separation. Be and I stopped talking for years. That happened in 1988, but we didn't speak again until 2001. In the late '90s, there was a P.M. Dawn website, and Prince Be would pop up on the forum. Eventually, I sent him a letter apologizing. Back then, he was a seventeen-year-old kid from Jersey struggling to get by. Really, I shouldn't have blamed him for wanting to leave."

The brothers were raised in a religious household, attended Catholic school, sang in church on Sundays, and that sense of spirituality spilled over into their music like forty days of rain: from *The Creation of Adam*/Sistine Chapel imagery of the cover of *The Bliss Album* to naming their third album *Jesus Wept* to Be giving out crosses to close friends and family. "I can remember him giving me a cross once," says writer/filmmaker Vivien Goldman, who first met the boys in London when she was hired by Jon Baker to make P.M. Dawn's video press kit. "I think we were at some gathering at Jon's house, and Be gave me a cross that he designed himself and had crafted out of heavy silver."

At the time, Jon Baker was married to Ziggi Golding, founder of the Z Agency, which repped models and photographers. Vivien Goldman worked with P.M. Dawn to get the duo ready for prime time. Through it all, Be and Jarrett kept their spiritual side in check, never slipping down slopes of coke, weed, or wicked women. "They were not very worldly when they got to London," Goldman continues, "and Jon and Ziggi took a caring interest in them. I filmed them a lot, but I was also their media trainer preparing them for interviews. Be was unconventional, but very natural and real, projecting a different sort of masculinity in living color."

When I asked Be about his religious views, he answered, "Well, we both went to Catholic school, but I learned more about religion from going to the library. I used to play hooky and go to the library. For me, reading was better than going to school." An avid reader, Be noted that a favorite book of his was *Jonathan Livingston Seagull*. "People always perceive Jesus as someone bigger than life, but they forget he was also a man. It's that people are afraid to find religion within themselves. People have to realize that they are important to themselves and to each other. That's the message I'm trying to get across. I found out last year that I have diabetes, and all of that has affected me as an artist. In terms of life and death, I believe in reincarnation; I just don't want to come back here."

In the U.K., Black Brits Jazzie B, A.R. Kane (can't nothing in the cosmos convince me that Prince Be didn't spend hours in his flat listening to the dreamy pop of *69* through Bose speakers), and Loose Ends were encouraged to be different, and P.M. Dawn was on that same vibe. England was the perfect place for them to be free. Be developed a studio relationship with engineer/instrumentalist (guitar mainly, but also bass and keyboards) Tyrrell as they worked out of Berwick Street Studios in London.

"Right from the first session for 'A Watcher's Point of View,' Prince Be and I got on extremely well," Tyrrell remembers. "I had just turned twenty-three, and we were just kids left on our own. The first session was such a success that we booked in for the rest of the album over the next three months. Jarrett was only really called upon when Prince wanted scratching and cutting on sections of tracks. Jarrett was a real master on the decks."

Although the brothers were new to London, there wasn't much time for sightseeing. "Since our time in the studio was so precious, the boys would come to the studio right after waking up and not leave until after midnight," Tyrrell says. "Prince Be had previously recorded demos of about half of the tracks, so he had an idea of some of the things that could be possible with sampling. I think my workflow speed and knowledge of the Akai S1000 sampler really opened his eyes a lot to new things that could be possible, which allowed for us to have much more creative freedom. Prince soon began to just play me three or four snippets off different records and asked me to make them fit together. He loved my 'Paper Doll' strings so much that every time after that when we wanted strings, he'd say, 'Let's use the "Paper Doll" strings.'

"We were soon experimenting with guitar parts over some of the tracks, too, like 'On a Clear Day' and 'The Beautiful,'" Tyrrell continues. "At first, he wasn't too keen on my suggestion to layer many tracks of his voice [something he called the 'Donny Osmond effect'] to create an ethereal vocal sound, but this soon became P.M. Dawn's signature. I would layer eight or more tracks on every harmony then sample and re-trigger them through the track."

After the worldwide success of "Set Adrift on Memory Bliss," the brothers were in France promoting *Of the Heart...* when they got a call from their management explaining that Eddie Murphy wanted to work with them. Although he

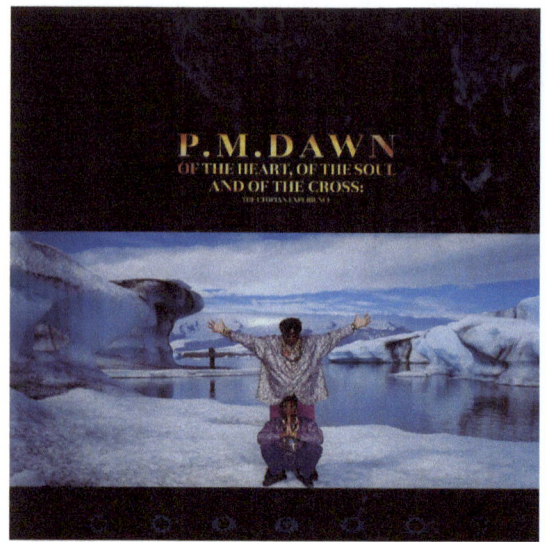

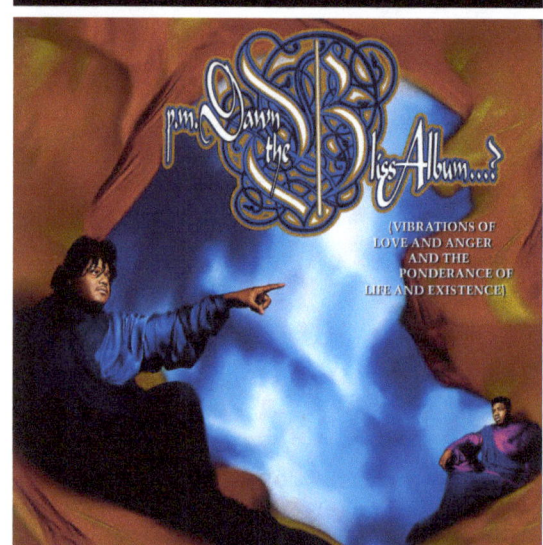
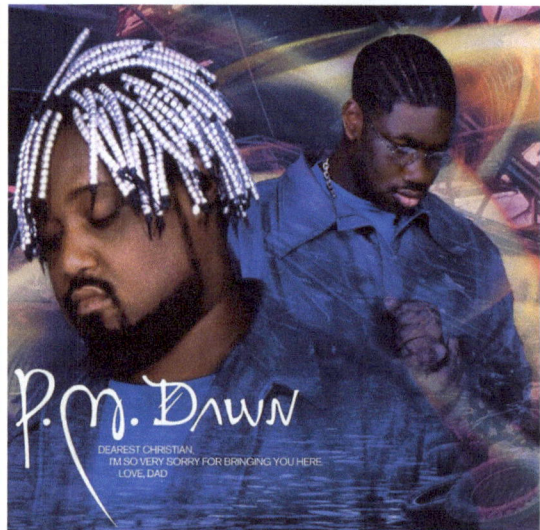
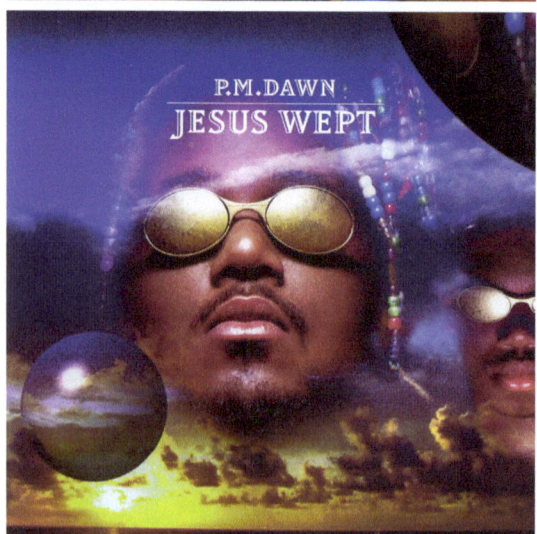
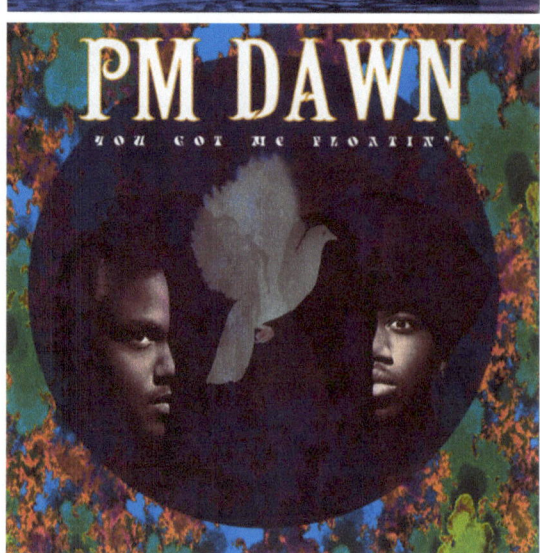

initially wanted them to contribute to an album project of his own, their meeting led to Murphy asking them to create a song for the soundtrack of his then-upcoming movie *Boomerang*. "Eddie told us that L.A. [Reid] and Babyface had the whole album locked down," Jarrett says, "but, if we gave him a song, he'd make sure it was on the record."

After returning to London, Prince Be summoned Jarrett to his room one night to share his latest inspiration. "Be was into Bobby Brown and Guy, but he had never written a straight R&B track," Jarrett recalls. "But, when I got to his room, he said, 'You're not going to believe this shit, but I did a fucking R&B song. He started singing the song ('Is it my turn, to wish you were lying here? / I tend to dream you when I'm not sleeping…'), and that was the beginning of 'I'd Die Without You.' We went to the studio [Strongroom] and started building the track with Tyrrell."

Tyrrell recalls, "I was always trying to convince Prince Be to do a song without any sampling, so the music for 'I'd Die Without You' started just from the chords I did on a synth-pad sound. The melody and lyrics he wrote over top were so great, as was his performance. I built up the song with programmed drums, synth bass, and some electric guitar, then we wanted live piano, so I suggested a colleague of mine, James Barnett, to come in and put down some dreamy improvisations down on the track. They even asked him to be in the video."

Graphic designer David Calderley, who began working with the group with his stunning cover for "I'd Die Without You," says, "Be was into the Storm Thorgerson album art for Pink Floyd, the Roger Dean paintings for Yes, and he wanted his own packaging to reflect that aesthetic. He had an affinity for the afterlife and cosmic experiences, and that became a part of the imaginary." Calderley designed most of P.M. Dawn's albums, singles, and CD art during their Gee Street period, with his last commission being their greatest hits package. "Prince Be would tell me his thoughts and overview, and I'd take his words and try to make it into a visual story. The only disagreement we had was the *Dearest Christian…* [album] cover, because, originally, the album had a different title."

Eddie Murphy's soundtrack song "I'd Die Without You" came out so well, P.M. Dawn had considered saving it for their second project; but, according to Jarrett, the Gee Street/Island Record executives weren't feeling it. "They said, 'You guys don't usually sing like that; where's the rapping?'" Jarrett recalls. "'You can give that shit to Eddie; we don't need it.' Of course, that record became a big hit and changed the sound of the group. After its success, we got a lot of flowers and apologies from the label. When we went to meet about the second album, they said, 'We need more singing. We even want ballads; let's get this shit going.'"

Returning to the Strongroom Studio with Tyrrell, who also received credit for his musical contributions to the project, *The Bliss Album* was their last collaboration with one another. "I was pulled from the mixing session due to disagreements between our managements and lawyers," Tyrell says. "This was a real shame, because Prince Be and I actually got on so well when creating together, and I felt there was so much more we could have achieved."

During the making of 1993's *The Bliss Album*, Be decided he wanted different scratch sounds incorporated into the tracks "Beyond Infinite Affections" and "The Nocturnal Is in the House," so he reached out to Philadelphia native DJ Cash Money and asked him to fly to England to work on the project. A few years before, the turntablist was signed to Sleeping Bag Records, where he'd released *Where's the Party At?* with MC Marvelous in 1988; but by 1992, he was spinning solo.

"Our mutual friend DJ Crash put us in touch," says Cash Money, whose latest album, *Street Cash*, was released in August 2018. "I had seen the 'Set Adrift' video and I figured, 'Ahhh man, let me go get this check.' I thought they were going to be some spacey dudes, but we just hit it off so great. They were just regular dudes, and when it was time for my studio session, I just went in there and knocked it out. I learned so much from Be about songwriting and layering voices. In the studio, he would just vibe out to the groove, and next thing, he would come up with a melody, build on that melody, and just start writing. He'd take it home with him and, next thing you know, he had a masterpiece."

Cash Money and Prince Be became so close that the DJ was asked to become a member of P.M. Dawn, which involved him touring with them and remixing the "The Ways of the Wind." The track was made into a video by a young Hype Williams. Film critic Armond White, who in 2006 presented the Williams retrospective *Believe the Hype: An Auteur Study of Hype Williams* at Lincoln Center, says of the video, "Hype is, of course, a genius. I can see what René Elizondo learned from that P.M. Dawn video (rhythm and color texture) and applied to Janet Jackson's 'That's the Way Love Goes' video the same year. Everybody learns from Hype."

Be saw himself as a "sampling artist," which meant that, like his new friend Cash Money, he was a crate digger who had a serious passion for record shopping. "We would go record shopping in London, but I knew a lot of the dealers personally, so we'd go to their house and buy records they didn't have in the store," Cash says. "Once, me, him, and Jarrett traveled for hours to a farm where the owner had the best record collection I've ever seen." Jarrett, too, remembers the trip well: "The guy had the records inside of a barn, and the entire barn, every inch of the place, was covered in vinyl. It was unbelievable. I thought Cash was going to faint."

Cash toured with P.M. Dawn, who had put together a band as big as Earth, Wind & Fire's that included backup-singing women and percussionists, and also appeared with them on

The Arsenio Hall Show, The Tonight Show with Jay Leno, and in the video for "Plastic." Rewinding back, Cash remembers, "We shot that under some bridge in New York and it was cold as shit. First, my jacket caught on fire, then the pigeons shit on me. I guess it wasn't meant for me to wear that jacket." But, whatever city they were in, Cash knew where to go buy records.

In New York City, Cash introduced Be to Roosevelt Hotel Record Convention where Q-Tip, Pete Rock, Large Professor, DJ Clark Kent, and countless others bought rare vinyl. If a bomb had fallen on that building back in the '90s, New York City hip-hop would've been over. "I introduced Be to a lot of the dealers, and Be's policy was never to haggle," Cash says. "He paid whatever they asked. He had money like that. If a dealer asked a $1,000 for the record, he'd give it to them. No bullshit, he would drop like ten Gs on records. Pete Rock and all those guys would be mad as shit, because the dealers would be holding special records for him. When we first started hanging, he was buying a lot of Blue Note records, but I schooled him on other things the same way he used to school me."

Writer, *Ego Trip* cofounder, and internationally known DJ Jeff "Chairman" Mao was a regular at the record conventions, and once sold Prince Be a copy of *Mark Murphy Sings* (arranged by Dave Matthews and featuring the Brecker Brothers and Dave Sanborn). "It wasn't a rare record; it went for about forty dollars," Jeff says. "There was a sense of resentment toward Prince Be from the other producers, because they didn't understand what he was doing with all those beats. I don't think many of them paid attention to his productions as well as all the songwriting and remixing he was doing."

Although P.M. Dawn often used musicians, sampling was a major component of their sound. Being a student and buyer of such diverse music gave Be a wider palette when it came to sampling. "In many cases, sampling artistry is still looked at as thievery," Prince Be said, "which was why we did 'Norwegian Wood' on the album." The song was released as a single with a video directed by future Wes Anderson collaborator Roman Coppola. "It's completely put together from samples," Be continued, "but it's a cover, so we didn't need permission to record it. I think sampling depends on a certain level of creativity. When EPMD sampled [Zapp's] 'More Bounce to the Ounce,' as much as some people thought that was thievery, I thought that was so creative, because of the way it was presented from a totally different perspective the original.

"Same thing with 'Set Adrift...,' because when it came out people said, 'Them rap kids stole from Spandau Ballet.' Even our record company thought we were a one-off until we delivered 'I'd Die Without You.' To me, you can't be a sampling artist and not be a hip-hop artist. I would never exclude myself from being a hip-hop artist. I just wanted hip-hop to be bigger than it was."

As much as Prince Be loved crate digging and recording, it equaled his disdain for being on the road. One night, he and Cash were in a studio in Los Angeles, and the DJ was supposed to drive them both to a show. "Be decided he wasn't going to go, because his psychic advised him not to. The manager was begging me to get him to the venue and I had to push his big ass into the car. I had rented a [Nissan] 300ZX and I literally had to push his big ass into the car and do a hundred miles per hour to get us to the venue. Luckily, I was only ten minutes late."

Released on March 23, 1993, *The Bliss Album...? (Vibrations of Love and Anger and the Ponderance of Life and Existence)* was another sonic marvel. "For me, the project possessed a dizzying array of aural vibes," says critic Quentin Harrison, "that includes funk ('So On and So On'), hip-hop ('Plastic'), pop ('About Love of Nothing'), and contemporary soul ('I'd Die Without You')." It remains one of the boldest and most flavorful records of 1993.

Although P.M. Dawn could've gone anywhere on the planet to live and work, the otherworldly brothers returned to their lives in New Jersey. Prince Be married Mary Sierra and settled in a Jersey City penthouse where engineer Michael Fossenkemper built him a portable studio. Fossenkemper, who had met the brothers the year before when he worked on parts of *The Bliss Album* out of his then-usual home-base Chung King. "That studio was one of those places where everybody kind of went through there," Fossenkemper says of the lab where Run-DMC, Brand Nubian, and RZA once recorded. "It was one of those places that many people ended up. It was popular in the hip-hop music scene." Fossenkemper, who had worked with Color Me Badd, was known for what he could do with vocals. "I think one reason Be liked working with me was because I had a lot of experience in harmonies and things like that. He really wanted to get more into that kind of thing."

In the beginning of the relationship, Fossenkemper was a bit baffled by Prince Be's work methods, not believing that certain samples or sounds would work or if his instructions were clear to the musicians. "After a while, I had to stop second-guessing him, because all his ideas worked," Fossenkemper says. "I'm convinced that he had the whole song recorded in his head already. He just needed someone to help him mechanically put it together. When I build the portable studio, I had an endorsement with Roland, and they came up with the DM-80, the first digital hard-disc recorder. It had eight tracks. I also had racks of samplers and a laptop with sequencing software.

"Be toured with the studio, but most of time we were working out of his place," Fossenkemper continues. "He converted a closet into a vocal booth. When you're at someone's house every day, you become like a member of the family. You watch the kids grow up, you're there for family arguments and the happy times. Every once in a while, especially if he was producing for someone else, we'd go to a conventional studio. You couldn't really ask Elton John to come to your house."

While Prince Be worked hard on the 1995 album *Jesus*

(top) Pete Rock and Diamond D check out Prince Be's digs at the legendary Roosevelt Hotel Record Convention in New York City.
(above) Prince Be with record dealer John Carraro. Photos courtesy of the John Carraro Collection.

Wept, he and Jarrett were also in the studio with artists he once worshipped from afar. "When we were in the studio with [Earth, Wind & Fire vocalist] Philip Bailey, he was schooling us on how Earth, Wind & Fire wrote songs together," Jarrett says. "Be and I would be sitting on the floor in the lotus position taking detailed notes. Then we were in the studio with Elton John working on his duets album. He thought Be was a great songwriter, so he gave us advice on how to further succeed and survive. When we worked with the Bee Gees, it was just weird having Barry Gibb asking us how we thought he sounded. It was weird, but we went there."

Fittingly enough, P.M. Dawn's cover of "You Got Me Floatin'" for the Jimi Hendrix tribute album *Stone Free* was recorded at the guitar legend's own Electric Lady Studios. According to Fossenkemper, "Be got selected for that project because [former Hendrix producer and engineer] Eddie Kramer, who spearheaded the project, picked Be because he like the way he panned on some songs. Eddie loved panning."

Releasing *Jesus Wept* in 1995, the brothers created an album inspired by heaven, love, and the afterlife as much as it was influenced by the Cali pop, Prince parables, and the Greenwich Village era of Bob Dylan. *Jesus Wept* combined cool existentialism, religious symbolism, and romantic ecstasy, and was exquisitely recorded at their home studio. The experimental and loopy album was on a mission to take hip-hop to new heights no matter how much the world resisted. With its blaring guitars (courtesy of Cameron Greider), retro go-go flow, graffiti-covered walls of sound, layered vocals, trippy lyrics, and the Holy Ghost floating above, the entire album was like a Victor Moscoso–illustrated acid trip in *Zap* comics that took the listener around the world in a day.

Jesus Wept was also a testament to Be's diverse sampling savvy as he mixed in beats ranging from Al B. Sure's new jack "Nite and Day" swoon on "Sometimes I Miss You So Much (Dedicated to the Christ Consciousness)" to Deep Purple's boogie "Hush" on the glam "Downtown Venus," the first single. "There's a solo on 'Downtown Venus' that Be helped pull out of me," says Greider. "It's crazy and over the top, but I never would've played it without his direction. Because of his sense of architecture, timing, and phrasing. He knew so much about constructing pop music and was a master without having an instrumental ability."

Meanwhile, showing that they could still swirl straight soul if need be, "Miles from Anything" has the appeal of a Delfonics/Thom Bell song while "Fantasia's Confidential Ghetto" partially covers Prince, the Talking Heads, and Harry Nilsson while throwing in some Charlie Brown cartoon samples as well.

In a four-star *Rolling Stone* review, it was written, "On their third album, P.M. Dawn completed their transformation from a rap-based pop group to something altogether different and wonderful. It's not that P.M. Dawn…don't operate in the hip-hop arena. Indeed they do. But…the duo has taken the sound of hip-hop so far beyond rap that it would be simplistic to discuss its music in those terms alone."

The album was released on October 3, 1995, but two weeks before it was due to drop, Jarrett was arrested on charges of aggravated sexual assault after allegedly having sex with a fourteen-year-old cousin. Although charges were eventually dropped due to lack of evidence, P.M. Dawn's reputation was tarnished regardless of the rave reviews the record received. Despite what Prince Be, Gee Street, or anyone else tried to do, *Jesus Wept* was overshadowed by the devil's mischief.

"For the record, my brother didn't rape anyone," Prince Be told *MTV News* in November 1996, "but my family is highly dysfunctional, which is the reason why I like to deal with the spiritual rather than the realistic." Four years later, P.M Dawn released their last Gee Street album, *Dearest Christian, I'm So Very Sorry for Bringing You Here. Love, Dad*, a disc that *Entertainment Weekly* writer Matt Diehl called "a truly ambitious pop album." Unfortunately, the project sank like a lead balloon and P.M. Dawn was dropped from the label.

In 2000, the brothers released *Fucked Music*, an album released on their label Positive Plain Music and only available through mail order. A few years later, as Be's sickness began to worsen, Jarrett began feeling as though he was having a spiritual crises and left the group to return to church. Having met Reverend Run when P.M. Dawn performed "I'd Die Without You" at his wedding in 1994, Jarrett went to the former superstar rapper for guidance. It was during that period that their cousin Gregory Carr began backing up the group under the name Doc. G.

In 2014, I spoke with Doc. G after I wrote an essay about P.M. Dawn for Soulhead. He told me he was one of Be's caregivers and that he had trademarked the group's name in his own name. It all sounded suspect to me, but as Anil Dash wrote on Medium.com, it only got worse: "Today, most of P.M. Dawn's social media presence is maintained by Doc. G, who also put out a handful of unremarkable releases using the P.M. Dawn name, with no apparent input from Prince Be. In the final half decade of Prince Be's life, Doc. G carried on the P.M. Dawn name (perhaps not entirely with the blessing of Prince Be's family, depending on the accuracy of online rumors), while Prince Be endured a further series of health setbacks. Another stroke, dialysis, and a leg amputation all took a heavy toll."

Since Prince Be's death in 2016, Doc. G has recruited a partner named K-R.O.K, and the two are conducting interviews and touring as P.M. Dawn. While this is a bizarre chapter in the book of P.M. Dawn, I doubt that this will be the end. Currently, Jarrett has been recording music for his purposed solo project, *Back to My Roots*, an album that will, in its own way, keep the musical memory of the original P.M. Dawn alive. ⭕

(*opposite*) DJ Minutemix and Prince Be of P.M. Dawn.
Photo by Chris Carroll/Corbis via Getty Images.

James Mason cut his teeth in the bands Tarika Blue and Roy Ayers Ubiquity before crafting his sole album, 1977's *Rhythm of Life*—a modern-funk monster and holy grail of record collecting—leaving a lasting legacy of his musical mind in just a short time in the industry.

Self Expression

by Allen Thayer

"I don't think I really believed it the first time I went to perform in England. I even suspected that it might be an elaborate practical joke," James Mason says about his three-night stint at London's famed Jazz Café in 1996. Following the reissue of his *Rhythm of Life* LP (originally released in 1977 and reissued in 1993), James received an invitation to perform his music for the first time in decades. "When we played some of the songs like 'Good Thing' or 'Funny Girl,' some of the slower songs, everyone was singing along. And that's when I believed they weren't faking it. You know, this could be one of those *Mission Impossible* plots where they stuff the place full of imposters. They could have been pulling hobos off the street, you know? But they all knew the words. This was for real." James took over the marquee from Al Jarreau, who only played for two nights. "I must be popular," he says.

(opposite) Image of James Mason from the 1977 album *Rhythm of Life*.

Fast-forward over twenty years, James is now James Mason, PhD, having completed his doctorate degree in socio-technical systems from the Stevens Institute of Technology and an MBA from Cornell University. Dr. Mason is excited to embark on his newly minted academic career as a development intervention architect, but he's continuously surprised and delighted by the enthusiastic reception of his musical past life. *Recollection Echo*, released in 2015 by Rush Hour records, compiles seven tracks mostly from James's demo tapes recorded in the half-dozen years following *Rhythm of Life*. The release approximates James's originally intended follow-up album that was going to be titled *Urban Bush Music*. In addition to two other vintage songs ("I Want Your Love" and "Nightgruv") released as a 12-inch single in 1996, James's limited but powerful body of work is unique in its marriage of warm analog sounds from 1970s jazz-funk with cutting-edge '80s technology, playing somewhere between the groove-based jazz of James's former boss Roy Ayers, the angular funk of Kraftwerk, and the adventurous sounds of Weather Report.

Born and raised in the Bronx, New York City, James chanced into music like many others, following in his older brother's footsteps by entering an after-school music program. His brother played clarinet, but after seeing the ways the girls reacted to the Beatles on *The Ed Sullivan Show*, James went for the guitar. "As I moved into middle school and high school and began buying my own records, rock and roll was a major influence," James said in an interview with this writer in 2013. "Aside from a serialized educational collection of selected symphonic classics that my parents subscribed to, Jimi Hendrix, Cream, and Led Zeppelin were among the first albums I ever bought. With the exception of Cal Tjader and the Palmieri Brothers, who I heard while visiting the homes of friends, I 'backed into' jazz through jazz fusion. While my high school peers were going crazy for Isaac Hayes's *Shaft* soundtrack, I was listening to the Mahavishnu Orchestra, the second Santana album [*Abraxas*], Jeff Beck's *Rough and Ready*, and Miles's *Tribute to Jack Johnson*."

While he wasn't aware of the influence at the time, Latin and Brazilian rhythms seeped into young James's subconscious: "Sergio Mendes on *The Ed Sullivan Show*. I remember watching Santana, Sergio Mendes, and the Beatles in the same month performing live on national television. I mean, that's pretty incredible, if you think about it." While in high school, and still years before James was composing and playing his own hybrid style, he played bass on some one-off gigs with Pucho and His Latin Soul Brothers, a Bronx-based Latin soul band that was one of a number of New York City–based bands mixing soul, funk, and Latin rhythms.

As a freshman at Hunter College in Manhattan, James was consumed by music. "They had concert-grade Steinways backstage in the auditorium, and I fell in love with the sound. I would spend hours back there instead of going to my classes. I would not say that I was a pianist though. Like many other musicians, I play keyboard to compose. I did fall in love with the synthesizer from the first time I heard 'Lucky Man' by Emerson, Lake & Palmer. To that point, I had never heard a sound that was anything like that. I was completely captivated. Synthesizers became an important part of my musical concept from that point on. Weather Report and Joe Zawinul later became a major influence beginning with the *Mysterious Traveller* album. It was total, passionate 'love at first listen.' Synthesizers were different back then. Today, synthesizers are a tool mostly used to recall a library of stock presets—and everyone uses the same sounds. I was attracted to the synthesizer because it was a way to invent a 'unique' situation-specific sonic atmosphere. Programming the instrument to develop the precise and singular sound was integral to the act of artistic creation."

Taking his education from the classroom to the road, James left Hunter College, spending what would have been his sophomore year as the baby-faced guitarist for Little Charles and the Sidewinders. "They initiated me into the musician's life on a chitlin circuit summer tour from Buffalo, New York, to Halifax, Canada," James recalls. "Charles was a consummate entertainer, and the band contained highly experienced sidemen who had worked with the likes of Otis Redding and Wilson Pickett. I recall the bass player had performed with the Jimi Hendrix version of the Isley Brothers for a short time. This was the university of R&B," he says. "I learned how to groove with those guys. I also got to hear a ton of great stories."

Back in New York, James soaked up the fusion of sounds that made the early 1970s such a creative period: synthspired prog rock, swinging salsa, spacey jazz fusion, and that funk thang seemed to stick to everything. James loved it all, but especially adventurous jazz fusion, which brings us to the band Tarika Blue. "I liked their sound immediately," James says. "I loved the song 'Blue Neptune' from their first album, because it reminded me of Zawinul and Weather Report—and I had never worked with a group that knew how to play that way before."

After playing with Tarika Blue for their self-titled second album (Ryo Kawasaki played guitar on their first album and split duties with James on the second), James joined up with Roy Ayers, first for a couple studio sessions before receiving an invitation to join the band in 1977. James is credited on Roy Ayers's albums *Lifeline* from 1977 and *You Send Me* on the song "Can't You See Me?" from 1978. "One of the big takeaways I got from working with Roy [was] the power of rhythm tracks," James says. "Among the musicians who I worked with back then, our favorite take would be the rhythm track. We'd listen to just the rhythm tracks. We'd cherish those tracks, because they had a certain openness—there's an incredibly compelling sense of purpose to the rhythm when it's in its bare bones. And if you didn't have that, you wouldn't finish building the song on top of it, because there was nothing there."

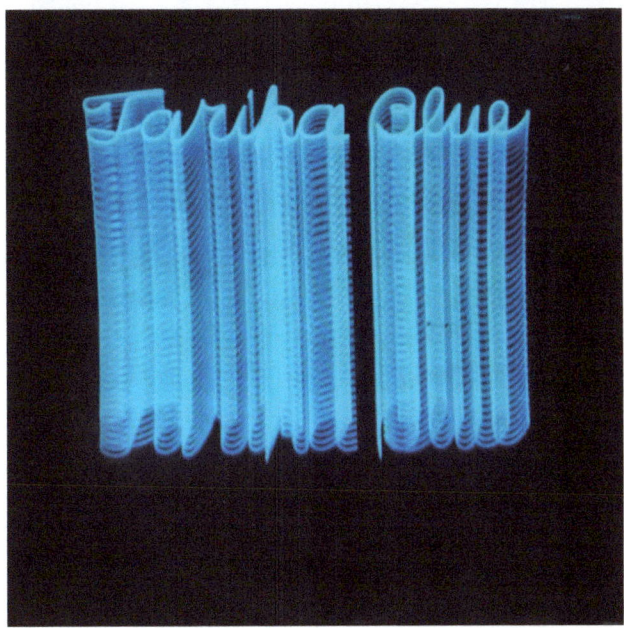

(*top*) James Mason (top middle) with Roy Ayers Ubiquity bandmates in front of the Nashville airport, circa 1977. (front row) Drummer James Bradley Jr., saxophonist Justo Almario, unknown friend, and trumpeter John Mosley. Photo courtesy of Philip Woo.

(*top left*) James Mason. (*top right*) Mason and *Rhythm of Life* singer Mbewe Ninoska Escobar. Photos courtesy of Philip Woo.

"My own music as a form of self-expression was always a dominant part of my musical persona," James said in a 2012 interview. "I had been a bandleader from my first garage band during my middle school years. When the opportunity to do my own album came along, as a twenty-two-year-old, I thought I was seeing my destiny unfold. It was everything I ever wanted to do, and I loved every minute of it. I immersed myself in the experience completely. I started writing 'Sweet Power Your Embrace' while I was on the road with Roy Ayers. I remember we were playing the Roxy in Hollywood. I went into the club during the afternoon when no one was around and worked out the basic idea on Philip Woo's rig."

James didn't just borrow his gear; as Philip Woo recalls, "I let him crash at my apartment many times." The longtime keyboard player for Roy Ayers and later Maze remembers contributing to James Mason's solo album: "I played on two cuts on the album, acoustic piano. When I recorded a piano solo, James had the drums muted, so I couldn't tell what the song felt like. When I heard all the instruments, it was totally different than I imagined!" he says. "James was a very interesting person—very cerebral, [a] deep thinker."

Working his connections and friendships, James recorded his 1977 solo album *Rhythm of Life* for $2,000 ($500 went to Narada Michael Walden for playing drums), mixing and mastering the songs in the middle of the night to save on studio costs. James had the whole album in his head, even the drum parts that Narada played. "What the kids would now call 'the beat,' I knew the kind of beat I wanted to have and how it was going to fit in with the other rhythm parts so that there's some kind of conversation between the rhythms. Narada hated me because I told him, 'Don't play that; play this.'"

"*Rhythm of Life* was and is a somewhat difficult work to categorize accurately, since it draws equally from several different genres and styles without fully belonging to any of them," DJ and liner-notes ace Greg Casseus explains in the liner notes for *Recollection Echo*. "This hybrid quality is usually hell on a record's commercial prospects but often ensures that it never goes away as future generations, equally versed in the different stylistic strains the music evokes, find their way to it." Tarika Blue's label, Chiaroscuro Records, was a jazz label and not to say that *Rhythm of Life* is not a jazz recording, but the album's lasting popularity (like contemporary releases from Roy Ayers, Donald Byrd, or many late-'70s jazz-funk masters) proves that its appeal extends well beyond listeners who consider themselves jazz fans. "It's that relatively rare work where every second counts and there really isn't a weak track to be found anywhere on it. It's almost as if five different imaginary Mason albums were mined for their strongest moments to make one perfect, solid ten-track album. Except that it is the actual album James made, straight to the point, all killer, no filler."

The album suffered the fate of many excellent albums recorded for the wrong label with little chance of wider success beyond adventurous radio and disco DJs. After the few sales were tallied, James managed to net a new winter coat for his blood, sweat, and tears. James continued recording his own work and playing with Roy Ayers and other jazz giants like Masabumi Kikuchi on two albums and Terumasa Hino on one.

James's transition to music education resulted from his passion and mastery of the new synthesizer technology. "I was always a big synthesizer guy," James says, gushing. "Love Josef Zawinul! In my apartment, I think I had two OB-8s, two [Yamaha] DX7s, a couple of DX9s; I was using Atari 1040ST computers linking those together; I was syncing to a VCR; and I had a La-Z-Boy recliner in the middle of the room. That was my living room of my apartment. I remember bringing a woman over and she goes, 'This is how you live? Where do I sit?'"

By the mid-1980s, James's bread was receiving more butter from his day job as a music educator than as a jazz musician and hustling solo artist. He describes two moments, or epiphanies, when he started to read the writing on the wall: "I was at Sweet Basil and saw Kenny Barron playing, who was at the time—in any genre—one of the greatest living pianists. It was a mid-week show, Kenny was approaching fiftyish, and I was a lot younger. He's playing with incredible subtlety. But everyone was talking and eating. I heard more dishes clanking than I did his piano. This was one of the premier jazz clubs in New York at the time, and even at that time he could only play there once or twice a year, and I said, 'Hell no.' There's no way I'm as good as this guy is, there's no reason to believe I would have a different fate, professionally."

The second moment came in a meeting in 1982 with some music industry big shots, pitching his follow-up album, to be titled *Urban Bush Music*. "Imagine if you fused Weather Report and Santana, and put the Pointer Sisters in front and make it a little funkier than either Weather Report or Santana, and there you go, that's it." In the mid-'80s, "urban music" was teetering between its disco past and hip-hop future. Russell Simmons and company turned the music business upside down with cheaper production costs and a street-team approach to marketing. As a relatively unknown artist, James knew his chances of securing the $20,000 he needed to make his demo were looking pretty slim. "That's when I felt it all kind of slipping away."

"I went into the Center for the Media Arts [in New York] and stayed there, trying to run away from what I saw as closing doors, because I wasn't very successful as a musician," James says. "Around the time, Soul II Soul was beginning to peak, and I remember feeling very unkindly about this second British Invasion," James says, not knowing then that the acid-jazz scene that Soul II Soul emerged from was influenced by his own music—and would be responsible for his musical comeback.

"James Mason's *Rhythm of Life* was certainly one of the key records that connected the rare-groove and acid-jazz scenes that emanated from the U.K. around 1985 to '90," selector

extraordinaire Gilles Peterson tells me over email. "Roy Ayers had been a staple artist with DJs like Froggy and Chris Hill who had a great influence on the U.K. jazz-funk scene prior to this time, and it was probably one of those guys…who might have discovered it and played it out first… [It's] difficult to say exactly who [rediscovered that record], but [it's] def a U.K. underground classic!"

Jazzie B Presents Soul II Soul at the Africa Centre (released in 2003) is a studio re-creation of one of the sound system's classic parties and, sure enough, James Mason's "Sweet Power Your Embrace" is on there. Along with, as Gilles Peterson recalls, "another song that would have been played in the same vein as 'Sweet Power' [which] was 'Music Is My Sanctuary' by Gary Bartz—both big Jazzie B tunes."

Meanwhile, back in NYC, and without the internet in the dark ages of the late '80s and early '90s, there was no way of knowing who was listening to or talking about James's music. "I think Jazzie B started listing me in his top ten list of influential artists," James remembers. "For a while, I was number one in his list of influential songs, but I think I've since slipped to number three." Then, a student of his who had previously served in the army was convinced he heard "Sweet Power Your Embrace" at discos while stationed in Germany. James still wasn't sure. "But then I would see in the back of *Billboard* magazine, they listed some club in Hong Kong's DJ playlist that read 'James Mason – "Sweet Power Your Embrace."' Who knows, maybe it's true?"

Based on his skepticism leading up to his Jazz Café debut in 1996, evidently even the offer to reissue *Rhythm of Life* in 1993 hadn't convinced James of his newfound following. In fact, James came to find out his album had a direct influence on Sade. "One of my coworkers from the early '80s was the assistant engineer at Compass Point when Sade did [1988's *Stronger Than Pride*]. Sade's song 'Paradise' might have been influenced by 'Sweet Power Your Embrace.' It's a short set of lyrics that repeat over a kinda funky bass line. I'm told that they definitely played my album in the studio, then played a groove, played the album—you know how they do to get the feel of a song?" Listening to the two songs side by side, the lines are not so blurry, but based on Sade and band's traveling in the same circles as Jazzie B and Gilles, it's entirely plausible that James's tune was in the recording studio with Sade and served as one of the thematic guides for "Paradise."

In the years since his musical renaissance in the mid-'90s, James Mason worked his way up the ranks at Panasonic and the NYSE, eventually running seven-figure budgets—all without

(top) WKTU radio station manager; Edwin Birdsong; unknown friend; and James Mason. Photo courtesy of James Mason. (opposite top) Roy Ayers Ubiquity bandmates backstage, goofing around on a tractor. (left to right) Saxophonist Justo Almario, conga player Chano O'Ferral, James Mason (in back with shovel), and drummer Jose Ortiz. Photo courtesy of Philip Woo.

a college degree—before finding himself decimated by the Great Recession of 2007–'08. In addition to pursuing an MBA followed by a doctorate degree, James also managed to excavate more tapes from the years after *Rhythm of Life*. When asked about the differences in instrumentation and sonic textures between his two "albums," James says, "Well, as opportunity declined, people stopped working with me," alluding to his increasing reliance on technology in the form of synthesizers and drum machines to complete his compositions. "I never wanted to do anything much more than my own music. I wasn't much good at doing anything other than my own music," James admits, acknowledging that his highly focused musical vision may have pushed some musician friends away. "So, consequently, I found myself by myself after some point."

Despite the music industry's disinterest in James's follow-up album over thirty years ago, the seven songs are far from cutting-room floor rejects. "What I come to realize most when I listen to *Recollection Echo* and imagine it together with 'I Want Your Love' and one or two other songs that I wasn't able to recover—my second album would have been pretty tremendous, especially if I had the chance to do it with the kind of quality production it deserved."

James Mason doesn't want your sympathy for the album that could have been, but he's genuinely moved that music fans like it. Talking to him for a few hours over Skype in 2015, he sounded positively thrilled about diving into his now-fourth career as a development intervention architect looking to systematically solve some of the world's challenging development conundrums using a new set of tools and technology. "To understand what I'm doing now," he says, "everyone should go to my web page [cornell.academia.edu/JamesMason] and download a copy of my article 'Social Enterprise Systems Engineering.' It's free and I get credit if you download it."

It's not that common to see creative types like James go on to successive successful careers after music, so I asked him what he thinks made him so good at his subsequent endeavors: "There's something that musicians and other artists have that people working a straight job don't typically have. To put it bluntly, they give a damn—passionately… Artists are used to being passionately engaged in what they're doing. Without the passion, it's not art. They really care and take a holistic view of the entire endeavor. It's as if you were a record producer, artist, and you're writing your own music. You care about the song, but you also care about the drum sound, the specific filter on the synthesizer—and the ambient sound design—all in context. In my experience, not a lot of people feel vested enough in what they do to bring that to the office. Transitioning from being an artist to an executive and now to an academic, I didn't know you weren't supposed to give that much of a damn. Being passionately engaged is fundamental to what it means to be an artist at work." ⭕

Magic Movement

Three free-spirited Brazilian musicians and a lyricist were put together by the hands of fate and men, namely Tom Zé and João Gilberto. Their ensuing band Novos Baianos might have been borne into the tropicália moment, but the group soon put down their own roots, making music on their commune-styled ranch. Despite initial resistance to their youthful, counter-cultural lifestyle and eclectic spiritual beliefs, Novos Baianos became one of Brazil's most-beloved bands.

by Joey Altruda

How could nine crazy hippies have any possible clue that the tunes they were tracking in their empty chicken coop would someday be seen as one of the most important albums in the history Brazilian music?

As many know, the music of Caetano Veloso, Gilberto Gil, and Gal Costa has widely become common knowledge over the years in the realm of "World Music," and in the past couple decades we could also add Tom Zé and Os Mutantes as being part of the nucleus that defined Brazil's tropicália movement of the late '60s.

This musical and social revolution was highly influenced by the Beatles' *Sgt. Pepper's* album and musique concrète, with a common thread being orchestrator Rogério Duprat acting as the George Martin role in creating the arrangements (with the exception of Tom Zé, who orchestrated his own music).

It's interesting to note that this movement was originated in Bahia and among the groups there is one in particular that is considered a national treasure, yet still remains widely unknown outside of Brazil (with the exception of some deep diggers). They are Novos Baianos. The music of Novos Baianos (New Bahians) was rooted in the tropicália/psych-rock scene, yet, under the mentorship and influence of João Gilberto, their sound morphed into something completely their own, something uniquely Brazilian.

(*opposite*) Crop of a photo from the insert of Mr Bongo's reissue of Novos Baianos' 1974 album *Acabou Chorare*. Photo by Antonio Luis (Lula), courtesy of Som Livre.

"At first, our music was very similar [to tropicália]," Novos Baianos singer/guitarist Moraes Moreira tells me, "but it was the influence of João Gilberto that really brought us into our own thing and set us apart."

I was first made aware of Novos Baianos through Seu Jorge, who showed me the 1973 documentary *Novos Baianos Futebol Clube* late one night at his Los Angeles home. It was like nothing else I'd ever seen before. I thought, "Who were these fascinating mystical hippies playing rock-infused samba?" I was completely enraptured and knew that these were my people, and that I must somehow find them. Serendipitously, four years later in 2016, I found myself on a plane to Bahia from Rio, traveling with the band to witness their first reunion show since 1997.

These two shows were not a mere "nostalgia revue" for fans from that generation by any stretch of the imagination. Conversely, the outdoor amphitheater was by and large filled with thousands of young people under the age of thirty, who sang along with every lyric to every song. It was a continuation of the strong youth movement that Novos Baianos had generated some forty-five years beforehand and a huge testimony as to the staying power and pertinence of their music. In a similar way that the Grateful Dead developed a decades-long following of counterculture, Novos Baianos has done the same (sans the avant-garde/space improv aspect).

To add a bit more perspective, in 1964, Brazil's government had been overtaken by a military dictatorship that lasted more than twenty years. People took to the streets in protest, many of whom were tortured, jailed, or even disappeared for being "subversive." It was a very difficult time for Brazilian life. Gilberto Gil and Caetano Veloso were targeted for such subversion and actually jailed for six months. After their release, they remained under house arrest for an additional

(*top*) Novos Baianos trio of singers (from left to right) Moraes Moreira, Baby Consuelo, and Paulinho Boca de Cantor. Photo by Antonio Luis (Lula), courtesy of Som Livre, from the insert of Mr Bongo's reissue of *Acabou Chorare*.

period of time before being deported to England, living in exile for two years. This would signify the end of the short-lived tropicália movement, which had only lasted approximately from 1968 to 1970.

Picking up the slack that was left with the absence of Caetano and Gil, Novos Baianos stood strong, smiling in the face of fascism and confusing the powers that be with their displays of overt joyousness and silent anarchism. They lived together on a ranch in the western zone of Rio de Janeiro where they spent every day for years playing *futebol*, cooking, studying metaphysics and spirituality, experimenting with hallucinogens, and changing the face of Brazilian Popular Music and youth culture. Their 1972 LP *Acabou Chorare* would define an entire generation and forty years later be cited by *Rolling Stone Brasil* as one the most important MPB albums of all time.

"We became the mouthpiece of a generation that yearned for freedom and certainly helped Brazil to emerge from this historically repressive moment," says Novos Baianos vocalist Paulinho Boca de Cantor.

The group was initiated by Luis Galvão in early in 1967, who found Moraes Moreira through the recommendation of Tom Zé. The eccentric artist Zé had a strong instinct that the pairing of poet/lyricist Galvão with singer-songwriter Moreira would be a great success on par with Tom Jobim/Vinicius de Moraes. As it turned out, he was spot on.

Galvão had studied engineering, graduated in accounting and typing, and worked in a marble mine that his father owned in Juazeiro. He met Tom Zé in his native land, the city of Irará, where Zé was working as an engineer, and, through their common passion for music, forged a friendship that has lasted a lifetime.

Upon first glimpse of his early lyrics, Tom clearly saw Galvão's raw talent and really felt that this fledgling poet could have a bright future as a songwriter.

Moraes first encountered Tom Zé while waiting for his course in medicine to begin at the University of Bahia, but was instead bitten by the music bug. At the time, Tom had studied composition, orchestration, counterpoint, musical analysis, and cello at the Music Seminary of the University and was giving private guitar and theory lessons. His fees were very expensive and it was clear by Moraes's poor rural clothing that he didn't have much money, yet he was insistent upon studying with Tom, stating that he too was a composer.

After hearing half a dozen original songs, Zé saw that there was the beginning of an artist inside Moraes and decided to teach him for free.

He taught one lesson a month, with very dense subjects, and when Moraes returned for the next lesson, he had everything transposed and repackaged, with several examples of composition, using the new resources.

"After two months," Tom Zé says, "I finished what I could teach, and he already played much better than me. Which made me very happy."

Galvão immediately moved into the same boarding house where Moraes and his brother were living, and by the end of two weeks, the pair had finished nearly a dozen songs. Soon after, they recruited singer Paulinho Boca de Cantor as another main vocalist and front-line personality. Paulinho had previously been singing international repertoire with the Avanco Orchestra, taking his stylistic influences from Nat King Cole, Sinatra, João Gilberto, Roberto & Erasmo Carlos, the Beatles, Jimi Hendrix, and others.

During this same time period, there was a local psych-rock band called Os Leifs (the Leaves) that featured brothers Carlinhos, Jorginho, and Pepeu Gomes. Pepeu was an outstanding young guitarist who idolized Jimi Hendrix and brought forth a noticeable star quality to the band. So noticeable that Gilberto Gil saw Os Leifs performing on TV, called the station to find out who this young talent was, and went straight to his home to offer him a job.

In 1969, just before Caetano and Gil left for England, there was a farewell concert in Bahia, featuring several groups—among them Galvao/Moraes/Paulinho and Os Leifs. That night, two worlds collided and it made sense that the initial crew bring Pepeu Gomes and his brother (drummer Jorginho) into the fold. A third, and very important key participant that evening was a ball of fire who sang with the ferocity of Janis Joplin and Elza Soares.

"Baby was introduced to us through our common friend Ediane Ferro," Paulinho Boca de Cantor recalls, "but we soon learned that she was a minor, that she had run away from home, and that her mother was looking for her. She had come from

(*above*) Novos Baianos woodshedding in the chicken coop. Photo by Mario Luiz Thompson.

Niterói, Rio de Janeiro. Her name was Bernadete Dinorah, but a character called Baby Consuelo in the movie *Caveira, My Friend* (from which we were making the soundtrack) inspired her stage name. Soon she conquered us, started hanging out, and then met Pepeu."

There was an undeniable chemistry culminating that would eventually lead to new sounds in Brazilian music.

"One day I went to Bahia to sing at a friend's house," Zé says. "Arriving there, I fell back, because I suddenly found the group of Novos Baianos fully formed. Moraes and Galvão met with Paulinho Boca de Cantor, Baby Consuelo, and sang songs that made me enthusiastic."

Now fully formed, the band performed in the 1969 show in Salvador, O Desembarque dos Bichos Depois do Dilúvio Universal, which was a stronghold of the Bahian intelligentsia. Novos Baianos played a very crazy set that left the audience appalled, sealing their fate that they would need to leave Bahia to find success.

Later, in São Paulo, Tom Zé was with his producer João Araújo (father of the singer Cazuza), and learned that producer Carlos Imperial had brought Novos Baianos to Rio and had left them stranded. Hearing this, he said to Araújo, "Look, I don't have the ability to give you professional advice about any band, but I beg you, for God's sake: listen to this band when you go to spend the weekend with your family in Rio." It was perfect. When João returned, he brought the group with him and took them to the businessman Marcos Lázaro. The next day they were singing on TV Record, which was the highlight of Brazilian music, beginning their professional career.

Their first album release, *É Ferro na Boneca!* (recorded in 1969 and released in 1970) mainly featured the vocals of Paulinho and Moraes, with nominal participation from Baby. Pepeu's guitar playing was prominently featured (he also played bass on some tracks), but the album was mainly comprised of studio musicians, with outstanding horn arrangements and organ playing by Chiquinho de Moraes. There was also one other arranger. At that point, they didn't yet have an entire band, only the singers, so Moraes collaborated with the arranger/maestro of the sessions, who based everything on his guitar concepts.

Novos Baianos had moved from Bahia to São Paulo and were residing at a hotel for a brief period, making television appearances and recording *É Ferro na Boneca!* They would soon find themselves living together in an apartment in Rio, in the neighborhood of Botafogo. Luis Galvão (the band's mentor)

(*above*) Baby Consuelo on the sitio. (*opposite*) Moraes Moreira. Photos by Mario Luiz Thompson.

thought it was of great importance to the band's creativity to cohabitate. One of the frequently mentioned stories of that era was of the epic futebol matches that they regularly held inside the apartment. The band had picked up two percussionists when they were living in São Paulo named Bola and Baixinha, plus dancer Charles Negrita, but they were still in need of a bassist who could handle Pepeu's intricate arrangements and the craziness of all the band members. This is when Dadi Carvalho entered the picture.

"I was at Arpoador with my friend, hanging out, playing guitars together on the beach," Dadi recalls. "Marilha [Moraes's then-wife] and Baby happened to come up to us and she told Baby that I play bass. They took me to the apartment where I met Moraes, Pepeu, and the others. At the time, I didn't understand their Bahian slang and accents."

During their time living together in the neighborhood of Botafogo, they were visited several times by João Gilberto, who had been friends with Galvão from when the two had lived in Juazeiro, Salvador. And as the famous story goes, the first time he visited the apartment, Dadi heard a knock at the door, looked through the peephole, and thought Gilberto was a police officer, immediately throwing everyone into a complete state of stoned-out panic.

Not a cop, João Gilberto rather enjoyed the company of these young crazy kids and loved to party with them, often playing music until daybreak the next morning. João had a dream of being part of communal living with music, and when he found out that Novos Baianos were all living together and making music, he sort of lived out his dreams vicariously through them.

When João first came to meet them, the first song they played for him was "De Um Rolé," plus some rock and roll, blues, et cetera. He said it was all right, but "you guys need to look into yourselves," meaning that they should really look into their Brazilian heritage. He wanted them to be more Brazilian so he showed them "Brasil Pandeiro," "Aquarelo do Brasil," music of Ary Baroso, and other classic Brazilian singers. At that time, Novos Baianos were more focused in international music and rock, so they began to change their sound, mixing Brazilian traditional music styles with rock instruments.

Gilberto's background had been in vocal harmony groups like Garotos Da Lua and Anjos Do Inferno. He loved vocal groups like Os Cariocas and would assign different vocal parts to the members of Novos Baianos. The song "Brasil Pandeiro" (originally recorded by Anjos do Inferno in the 1940s) would later become one of their signature tunes and a Brazilian

anthem. In fact, they personalized the song to such an extent that most people think that they wrote it.

"He would play the guitar for us, using his own special chord voicings that we'd never seen before," remembers Moraes of João. "Pepeu and I would watch him intently, studying what he was doing, and as soon as João would leave, we would ask each other, 'How many did you get?' Pepeu: 'I got six.' Moraes: 'I got five.' And then we would play them and compare notes. That's how we learned the vocabulary of bossa nova."

It was also João Gilberto who gave Moraes the book of Yogananda, *Autobiography of a Yogi*. This was the book that really guided the spirituality of Novos Baianos. They were influenced by all the major Indian gurus. Baby was very spiritual and, for example, if the car broke down or ran out of gas, she would take a piece of spiritual fabric, place it on the car and believe that their spiritual energy would fix the car. They would read the Bible, and, to them, it was apocalyptic. One day, they saw a big black cloud and believed that Christ would descend from it.

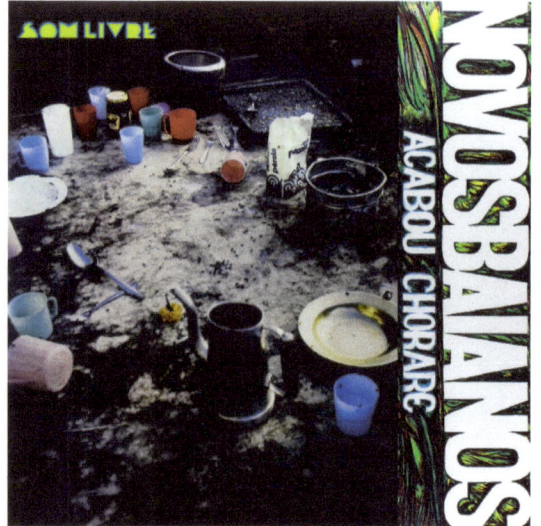

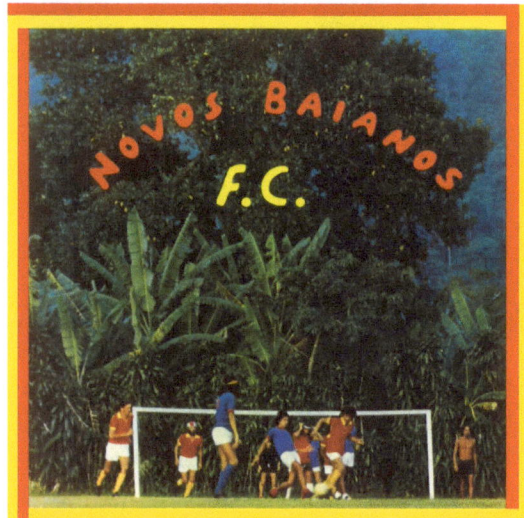

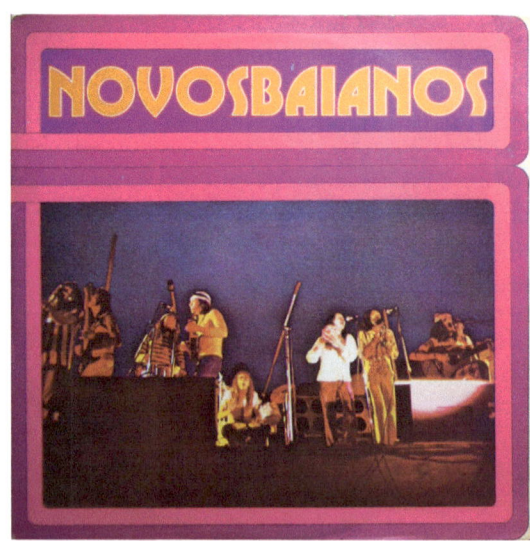

✪✪✪✪✪

Acabou Chorare, the band's second release, showed a radical change in the band's sound. They took heed in João Gilberto's tutelage, combining elements and influences of frevo, bossa nova, samba, baiao, among others, with their already hard-rockin' sound. Pepeu's secret weapon was a custom-made distortion pedal made from Baby's television set. She had bought the TV to watch the World Cup, and one day came home to find it broken, but couldn't understand why it wasn't working.

"There was a guy living with us on the *sitio* named Salmão, who was like 'the MacGuyver of electronics,'" Moraes says. "He removed the tubes from the TV and made the distortion pedal. It was Pepeu's idea, but it was Salmão who built it."

It was during this same time of change that the band moved to a sitio (ranch) in the west side of Rio (Jacarepaguá), where they could live together without the constant headache of being hassled by the authorities for being hippies. It was a sprawling area, with up to forty people living there at once according to Gil Oliveira (current Novos Baianos percussionist and son of Paulinho Boca). They even formed their own futebol team, which played proper matches and had several professional ringers, plus other big celebrity members such as Chico Buarque, for example.

According to the band members, the futebol actually took precedence over the music. The youth at the time, disillusioned by the state of the governmental dictatorship, felt a kinship with Novos Baianos, their music, lifestyle, and outlook on life, and began following the band in large numbers. It was a very dangerous period of time. There was a lot of repression coming from the authorities who suspected people of being communists, but they looked at Novos Baianos and thought that "these people are way too crazy to be communists."

"It was commonplace to be stopped and frisked by the police on the streets because we had long hair," Moraes recalls. "We finally left the city to live together on the sitio, where we could be left alone."

Instead of following fashion, they invented it. They had their own slang, in tune with the youth of the time exercising mysticism, zen experiences, and alchemy, all with a spirit of anarchy and positivity. Also hallucinogens, which played a significant role in the spiritual aspect of the band and their songwriting.

"We faced repression as if in a game of futebol, giving blood, sweat, intelligence, calm, youth, soul, and other virtues to win," Galvão says. "Of course, also, we had losses, but we members believed that we had a mission."

Side note—one side of the *Acabou Chorare* LP was recorded in a studio in Rio; the other side was recorded at the sitio, where they had converted the abandoned chicken coop into a home recording studio. It had good natural acoustics so they

(*opposite*) Novos Baianos in the studio. Photo by Mario Luiz Thompson.

cleared it out and equipped it with a Teac four-track tape deck and not much else (no acoustical treatment for example, only their amps).

Paradoxically, the police also were fans of Novos Baianos. Sometimes, the band would show up to the sitio and a cop car would be parked in the entrance.

"We would be freaking out," Moraes remembers, "thinking that we were going to get busted or something, when all the cops really wanted was to hang out and talk to us." He laughs. "It was really magical."

In 1973, a German TV company hired Solano Ribeiro to direct a documentary about anything he wished in Brazil, so he chose Novos Baianos. The outcome was *Novos Baianos F.C.* (Futebol Clube), a forty-three-minute film that depicts their daily lives together living on the ranch, making music, playing soccer, raising their children, cooking elaborate communal meals, and sharing in their philosophies of life.

At the time, aside from Germany, it was only aired on a couple Brazilian TV channels, but in recent years has been widely circulated on the internet. To look at it now, there is a certain haunting aspect to it because of the faded graininess of the actual film, but also because of the time capsule that it is. It's cinéma vérité at its finest, and the depth of candid joy and love really shines through, especially taking into account the dark times Brazil was then faced with. The audio was recorded on a Nagra tape deck (the highest quality/industry standard portable reel-to-reel tape deck at the time), and they only used one ambient boom mic and one hand-held mic for the vocals, yet miraculously, you can hear everything, even the acoustic guitar.

"It was very cool to experience," Paulinho Boca says. "We lived together at the ranch in Jacarepaguá and managed to show the philosophy and way of life that charmed everyone. We were a tribe playing with peace and love. And the fact that we recorded live on a Nagra recorder with a single microphone showed an extraordinary performance, a result of the wonderful moments we spent living together in a community, making music, and playing futebol."

In 1974, Moraes made the difficult decision to leave the band and embark upon a solo career. At that time, he and his wife had started having kids, and the living situation on the sitio was far from optimal for them. They didn't always have money; there were always people coming and going; and sometimes they didn't have basic things like milk for the children.

Among all of them, there was no one with the talent to organize the living logistics. According to Moraes, Marilinha (Paulinho's then-wife) did her best for a long time. She really tried. And whenever a new band manager would come into the picture, he would try to organize everything but would end up falling into the craziness of everything and forget about his job as a manager.

Dadi followed suit soon after, taking employment as bassist with Jorge Ben (first appearing on Ben's *Africa Brasil* LP in 1975). Pepeu's younger brother Didi (then seventeen years old) took up the bass chair in the band and Novos Baianos went on to make four more albums and live on the sitio until 1978. At this point, Paulinho Boca de Cantor went on to a solo career as did Baby and Pepeu, who became two of Brazil's biggest rock stars of the '80s. They married, had six children, and remained together for twenty years.

The band reunited briefly in 1997, releasing a live album entitled *Círculo Infinito* (Infinite Circle) but remained dormant for another nineteen years because of everyone's busy solo careers. In May 2016, under the coordination of Pedro Baby (son of Pepeu and Baby), Novos Baianos took to the stage once again, embarking on a nationwide tour agenda that has been going strong ever since. Their live DVD/CD release, *Novos Baianos Se Encontram* (on the Som Livre label), recently won them two Premios (the Brazilian equivalent of the Grammy) in the categories of Best Rock/Pop Act and Album of the Year.

The year 2019 marks fifty years for the band, with plans of a new studio release commemorating their Golden Anniversary and a strong vision of touring abroad for the first time.

"We put all our lives as young revolutionaries in this work," Paulinho says. "We believed that we were changing the world, and we dreamed of a better world, even knowing that the system is gross. And today we see how important it was to have dreamed and fulfilled our dream. We helped the world to dream of a time of peace and love and we're still dreaming. We cannot stop dreaming." ○

The Golden Touch

by A. D. Amorosi

French drummer and producer Marc Cerrone embraced synthesizers, drum machines, and primitive sequencers to create disco gold like "Supernature." Its success allowed the hitmaker great freedom to explore dance music's different colors. Even after the downfall of disco, the sound he helped create went underground and only got bigger, while Cerrone himself has continued to be productive and prolific both in the underground and mainstream.

"I think my new stuff is right on time, you know, having a good bass gimmick like I always had," says Marc Cerrone—known singularly as Cerrone. The disco era's most soulful and preeminent Franco-Italian drummer, composer, and producer, whose ongoing work in organic analog material is as bold as his electronic schematics, Cerrone is talking and laughing about his first major-label American album in a minute, the brisk, tech-y, tribal-inspired *Red Lips*, released in fall 2016. "The power of the rhythm is there with the big beat, probably bigger than before, because that's the thing now. So, maybe the melodies are different now and today's songs have a greater number of words—maybe too many words on a track—but this is very much me. What did you expect?"

(*opposite*) Cerrone and friends. All photos courtesy of Cerrone.

Following hot on the heels of his pulsating *Afro* EP, *Red Lips* includes guests such as Nile Rodgers, Aloe Blacc, Kiesza, Yasmin, Alexis Taylor of Hot Chip, and Fela Kuti drummer Tony Allen—the last of whom was a big part of *Afro* as well. "I am humbled by all my good company," Cerrone says of his lively album, speaking about its visitors as if it was a decadent dinner party. But, *Red Lips* is one chef and one host—all Cerrone—with dense drumming, thick, jumpy bass lines, and sensual melodies that will remind you of his careening dance-floor classics, such as the elegantly dirty "Love in C Minor" and the jittery "Supernature," without clinging to the past, his own or the heralded era from which they came. "The next time we speak, we will do so through red lips," he says with a hearty chuckle.

Unlike the other boldly notorious and well-loved Franco-Italian disco-era composer and producer, Giorgio Moroder, Cerrone never retired or even disappeared from plain sight. Though he slowed his record-release roll in the 1990s—opting mostly for electronic-based soundtracks for several French films, and he even wrote the music (and the original story) for a 1992 Broadway show, *Dreamtime*, with an accompanying CD release, *Dream*. Cerrone did more remixes then than Diplo does now. "Especially with my own music, as I love the new technology and where I could take things," he says. "I always did love the technology, though—that's what made 'Supernature' super."

Cerrone too carried on throughout the '90s and early 2000s with massive live productions abroad: a 1996 light show for the Dalai in Nice; a 2005 free concert at the Palace of Versailles, which he once called "the biggest discotheque in the world"; and in America, 2008's Times Square Dance Party with Nile Rodgers. Yet, he never stopped putting out new music, demonstrated by sinewy, European-only releases such as 2007's *Celebrate!* and the single "Love Ritual" with Louie Vega.

"America though—New York, Atlantic Records—was everything to me when I first started making records," he says wistfully. Hence the importance of *Red Lips* beyond its continuation of the Cerrone brand. There's the gloriously sexual humanization of the electro-disco pulse with his insistent fleshy feel for deeply grooving drums, orgasmic wordless coos, or bluntly put lyrical concepts (at least where "Supernature" was concerned), and the shimmering real-time feel of strings and horns so prevalent in vintage American R&B, soul, and rock. "It is true, Barry White and Chicago were as important in terms of influence as was, say, Hendrix."

What influenced Cerrone from the start, however, was the drum—at first subtle and jazzy, eventually deeply grooving and even thundering at times. "Oh yes, I banged on everything," he remembers, "many, many desks and tables in school. I was not a good guy because I painted on the tables and drummed on the tables. So I was asked to leave school more than one time."

Cerrone's mother had an idea. While neither she nor Cerrone's father were keen on their son playing an instrument ("At least not drums, no, not keen, as you say"), they offered the youth a compromise: pass school and get good grades, and at the end of the year, they would buy him drums. "I said, 'Wow, what a strange idea. Okay, let's do that.' I passed all my classes and she bought me my drums. It was the first of many happy accidents in my life. You will see as we talk."

Fond as he was of all Black music—mentioning specifically Jimi Hendrix, Sly Stone, Santana, "the whole of the Black Woodstock nation," as he sums up—the young Cerrone played in small ensembles throughout France, inspired by American rock and roll and R&B and African rhythm. "Never French music," he says with laughing disdain. "*Nooo*, it never spoke to me. Maybe today, because all music is international and more rhythmic. But if I had to have only played French music growing up, I probably would have stopped making music."

One enterprise that opened his eyes to broader productions and bigger arrangements was Cerrone's first real employment at age seventeen: convincing Club Med cofounder Gilbert Trigano to let him curate and book bands for his cruise line and vacation stays.

"Yes, that is true. My father had asked me to work while I was in school—I was fine with that—but I also wanted to be a musician, so I said no to convention. We had a fight and I left, which meant I had to find a home. Now to soften the blow, I had to find a girlfriend, preferably older, with an apartment. I found one of course—ha ha ha—but two years later, she was going to leave and pack up her apartment so she could work for Club Med. I went with her to the going-away party, and the guy who owned the ship came to me and said, 'You look so sad. Why?' I told him that 'You're taking my girlfriend, and I don't know where I will live now.' He asked me what I did, and I said music, and we got to talking about me finding musicians and singers for tracks for the trip. Lots of big sounds was my idea. He went, 'Wow,' and that became the true beginnings of me taking control over a sound. And, another [happy] accident, I might add."

Stepping back to the idea of rhythm being the driving force in Cerrone's life, musical or otherwise, is what led Cerrone to his first real compositional project, Kongas—a band who played progressive, polyrhythmic, Fela Kuti–inspired Afro-funk at the Papagayo club in Saint-Tropez, France, in the early '70s. Pushed to chart stardom by French producer and label owner Eddie Barclay—who signed Kongas to his Barclay label—and buoyed by the early success of singles such as "Boom" and "Anikana-O" (cowritten with his pal, Alec Costandinos), Cerrone still speaks fondly of his start as a composer.

"The six of us composed as a team, mostly. I learned like that, how to orchestrate, on the job. And we had a lot of success between 1972 and 1975. *Afro Rock* [Kongas' 1974 debut album as titled in the U.K.] still sounds great. But, you know, after

(opposite) Cerrone (center front) with his band Kongas, 1972.

three years, that wasn't the music I wanted to make any longer, so I left. That was the end of the dream as a musician, but the beginning of my life as a producer."

This beginning ("So many beginnings, no?" he giggles) also came courtesy his Kongas pal Costandinos with whom he wrote a sensuously epic track the likes of which had not been heard at that time. "Because it was too long," says Cerrone, "no record label would touch it, because they could not put it on the radio. That wasn't the point. I didn't write it for the radio. I wrote it for the dance floor."

Cerrone is talking about his 1976 debut solo effort, *Love in C Minor*, which he eventually released on his own Malligator imprint that he had pressed in London. "I got some friends together and we put our money on the table," he says. "I thought I was going to sell two copies... I mean, this music was for me, what was in my head." Arming himself with five thousand copies of the records to start, Cerrone sold *Love in C Minor* in dribs and drabs until one of the stores he was dealing with accidentally sold copies of it to a shop in New York City. "Uh-oh," he laughs, noting yet another fortunate accident.

Suddenly, everyone in NYC was looking for the guy who made this intense, swirling dance music who dared to put nude women on the cover ("Oh yes, the ladies, that became a signature of mine"). Yet, he was impossible to find, as its original pressings came with no ID beyond the naked flesh. "Funny thing was, [Casablanca boss] Neil Bogart told me this great story about trying to reach me. He thought we were in London because of the record's pressing." It wasn't Casablanca that found Cerrone, however, but rather Atlantic's Cotillion division and its legendary overseer Ahmet Ertegun. Costandinos pretty much left Cerrone around the same time to create "I've Found Love" by Love & Kisses and the disco opera version of *Romeo and Juliet*.

"A friend of mine told me how popular 'Love in C Minor' was there, which I thought was impossible, so we went to New York to see so for myself. And the first person I met with was Ertegun," says Cerrone. "He thought my being anonymous was funny. He loved the record. He wanted me to be his next big arranger-orchestrator. That was something. So we changed the cover to include me, released it, and this was all a success."

Starting from 1976, Cerrone moved to the United States, first NYC then Los Angeles, as Ertegun wanted the producer-composer to do even more work in the bourgeoning disco era. "I accepted that invitation with pleasure," Cerrone says. "I liked it so much, I wanted to bring my family over, so Atlantic bought a house for me in Los Angeles. My old contract was great. I liked being with them so much I re-signed with them now."

Calling the success of the grand *Love in C Minor*—its titular single sold three million copies—another happy accident in his life, Cerrone insists that he wanted to see what he could do on purpose. That's where *Cerrone's Paradise* came in. While the 1977 French album cover welcomed a naked model draped over a fridge with white powder spilled on its floor, the American release featured a photo of Cerrone wearing a Hawaiian shirt—with his famous mustache intact. The only thing more famous on the covers of Cerrone's albums other than the female form ("That was nice, no?") was his mustache. "Oh my, you love my mustache," he roars with laughter. "It was good. I think I only grew it because it was a thing, you know? Like tattoos are now. It was distinguished."

So too was *Paradise*. Along with its more epic, hornier sound (literally and figuratively), and its denser, more swelling string orchestrations, Cerrone began producing quiet-storming, sultry-soul stuff like "Time for Love" as part of its wall of sound. "I produced what I loved, and to me, after *C Minor*, I really wanted to prove myself," says Cerrone, citing Barry White as a huge inspiration on that album's soaring sound. "*Paradise* was a big deal to me. It was also the last of its kind, and I knew it."

Around the time that *Paradise* was coming out, Cerrone discovered synthesizers, drum machines, and primitive sequencers, and he enveloped those in a concept of submerging his symphonic dreamscapes with the icy cool and rigidity of the synthesizer. "This was a revolution to me, and I loved it. Between this and meeting this crazy girl Lene Lovich [a new-wave singer who wound up writing eco-conscious lyrics for "Supernature"], I was changing. I thought Ahmet would love this—I was confident—but remember he thought of me as the next big orchestrator in his life. He was not so, how you say it, keen."

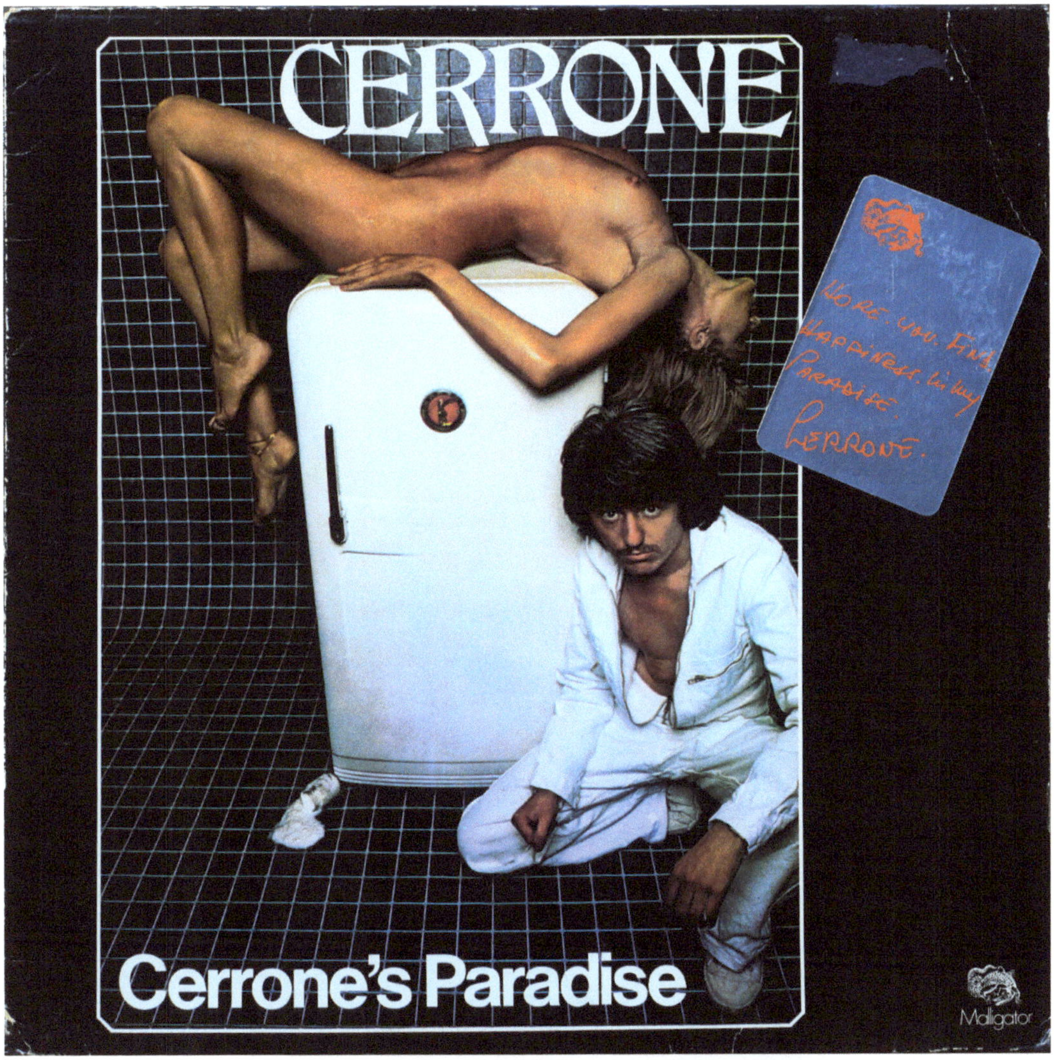
CERRONE
Happiness. in my
Paradise.
Cerrone.
Cerrone's Paradise
Malligator

CERRONE
CERRONE'S PARADISE
Promotional
Copy
NOT FOR SALE

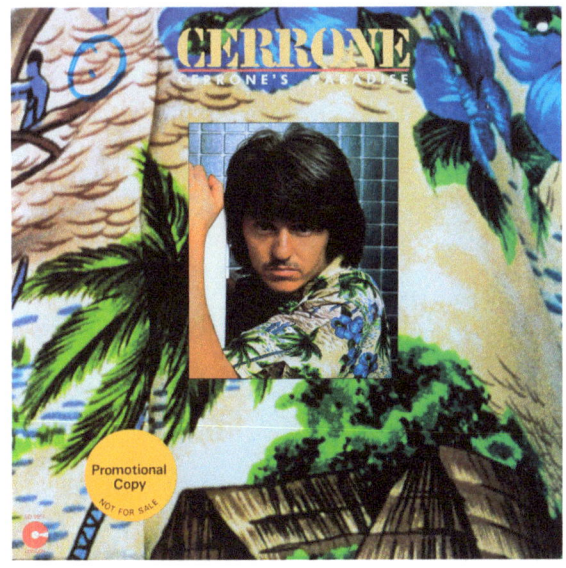

Love it or not, arguments aside, Cerrone was going forward with 1977's *Supernature*, a still-dramatic merging of organic-horn and string sounds with the pulsating, arpeggiating synthesizer. "I think Ahmet wound up happy that I pushed him, because we sold over eight million copies. After that, he was like, 'Do whatever you like.'"

What *Supernature* did was span the vanguard of both new wave and where disco was at that moment, yet still stretching miles ahead. Along with maintaining warmth and emotion in its real strings and horns, Cerrone's drive toward the synthetic was welcome too, as he "added animal sounds to make it more me—*ha ha*—and then the Lene Lovich thing." Considering that songs with words for the dance floor weren't a thing to be done, the eco-consciousness of saving the planet was a big deal. "I mean, nobody was talking about that then. Nobody had heard this—a message—on a dance record. Plus, she was a punk princess and this was disco. It was all very funny."

Cerrone never had a problem with the word "disco" or building upon its enterprise. Successful as he was, he stuck with that synth-organic instrument mix, eventually morphing more toward the former and eventually usurping his creativity with *Cerrone VI* being more of an electronic soundscape ("I liked the Fairlight," he says, referring to the famous synthesizer) rather than a dance record. Until then, however, *Cerrone IV: The Golden Touch* and *Cerrone V: Angelina* were disco, simple, pure, and gloriously unadulterated—à la "Je Suis Music," "Look for Love," and the R&B-ish "Rocket in the Pocket." Yes, the latter album had elements of jazz-fusion in its mix, but this was disco at its peak.

"At that time—'76, '77, '78—you're having success," he explains. "You try to stay with it, but you also want to satisfy yourself. Remember, when we started, disco was still very underground. It became huge, and pop, only after *Saturday Night Fever*. I liked it being underground. After *Fever*, it was all downhill. As a producer, I was always trying to create an atmosphere. You couldn't do that in three minutes and thirty seconds. That's no place for atmosphere, no build. What I do now is still disco, but like every other electronic music—garage, house, techno, electro, EDM—every style has to have that large, hard rhythm track; a big beat that makes people happy. It's always cheery now. Not underground either, something else."

Cerrone V went for something else indeed, as it marked the drummer-producer's first shot at singing—another accident, as he created guide vocals for another crooner at album's start. "Why not, you know," he laughs. "Plus, I wanted to show the record company that I could do [it]." That same *V* album also featured members of Toto—Boz Scaggs's one-time contributors—and the start of Cerrone's Los Angeles period. It also marked the end of his tenure with releasing albums in the U.S., as 1980's *Cerrone VI* (subtitled *Portrait of a Modern Man*) was a Euro-only release that marked his first, full-on foray into electronic mood music.

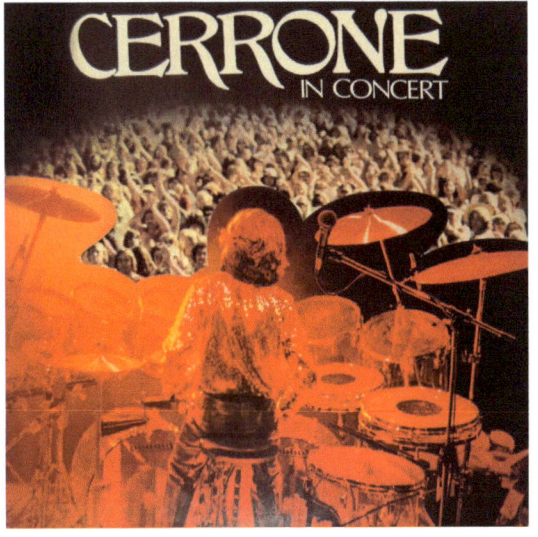

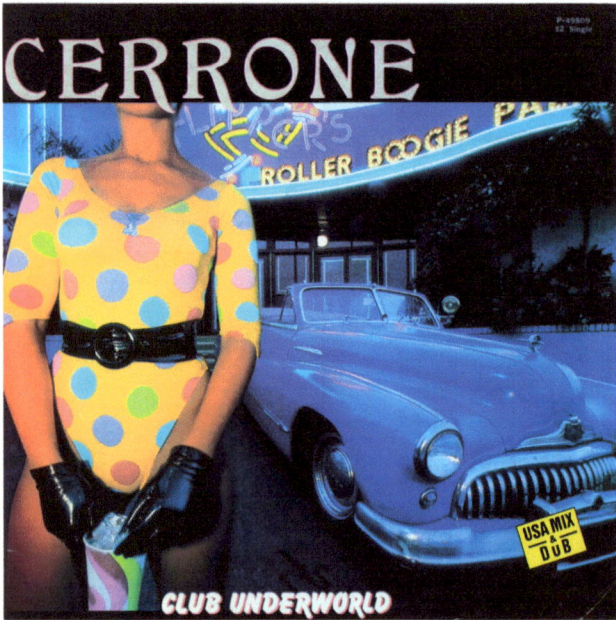

That same year marked the start of his crafting compositions for foreign film soundtracks (*Super Witch of Love Island* aka *Vaudou Aux Caraïbes*) that continued through the early 2000s with the soft porn *Emmanuelle 2000* series. "Oh yes, that was nice," Cerrone says blithely. By 1983, rather than eschew hip-hop, as much of disco's production elite had, Cerrone embraced it on the appropriately titled track "Club Underworld," from the album *Where Are You Now*.

Again, Cerrone points out how rap and hip-hop culture at that stage was still in its nascent stages, and fascinating to him. "From my point of view, it was not as big then as it is now; still very much under the radar, so I use that—and used it sparingly—because, quite frankly, there are far better producers of that than me. I stay in my place. I love to hear it. I just don't feel strong enough to concentrate on that, so I do my soul, my funk, my techno."

Along with crafting a small, still sensuous, and steely klatsch of original-artist albums within the last twenty years, Cerrone has concentrated on live spectacles throughout Europe and remix after remix of his classic material, most of which he has either made himself or approved of and still adores. "The orchestration has mostly been the same. Just how much are you going to take away? We changed the world in the discotheque—the electro, the orchestration—made dance music with real strings and guitars. Maybe today there are more computers, but," he insists, "it is always about good grooves and good atmosphere."

This brings Cerrone to the *Afro* EP, done mostly in tandem with Tony Allen—Fela Kuti's most favored drummer—then *Red Lips*. "I love and respect Tony's drumming, as it feels so much like my own," says Cerrone when it comes to the EP and Allen's contribution to *Red Lips*, "2nd Chance." Again, Cerrone takes another dip into soft hip-hop waters with "C'est Bon" with gentle rapper Aloe Blacc ("I could not resist," Cerrone insists), with the rest of *Red Lips* regaling in high-energy anthems and deep, huge beats.

"That is what people like—it is what I like," he says enthusiastically. "For me to get back to the studio, it depends, you know, I have to excite myself. During the '70s, it would take me many months to come up with something—half a year, maybe—but today, you cannot wait that long to invent it and get it out, because it will sound old. I like the new style and moving fast."

Never taking it slow, Cerrone is starting the new decade with a primal scream via the release of yet another new full-length opus, *DNA*. Cerrone's first entirely instrumental album and a welcome return to an all-electronic music format of the past, *DNA*'s first singles, "Experience" and "The Impact"—a progressive house cut featuring a sample of animal scientist Jane Goodall—find its footing in the environmental messaging that was "Supernature," his most highly touted hit. ○

On That Other Level

Rap-A-Lot Records bubbled up in Houston, Texas, with founder James Prince's Ghetto Boys holding things down. But with a name and lineup change and a focus on hard-core lyrics à la NWA—and with a little help from producer Rick Rubin—the newly minted Geto Boys put the label and its city on the hip-hop map.

by Dean Van Nguyen

Houston, as it turned out, was a sleeping superpower. A dormant Death Star just waiting to fire up its heavy machinery and soar onto the hip-hop landscape. New York was the birthplace. California is where they put their mack down. But the South hadn't yet decided what it wanted its rap scene to be. The cache of wildfire was primed to explode underneath H-Town. All it needed was somebody to light the touchpaper.

As fate would have it, that very person was residing in the Fifth Ward. Born in 1964, James Prince came up in an area notorious throughout Texas for its violence and destitution. Thirty-four percent of the population lived below the poverty level. It was a neighborhood described in a 1979 *Texas Monthly* article by Richard West—as an outsider looking in—as being like a whole "new country" with "a different language, a different skin color, a different set of values, a different family structure, and its children play different games…. It is a cryptic, closed society existing in the middle of Houston."

(*opposite*) The Geto Boys in 1990: (left to right) Akshen aka Scarface, Bushwick Bill, DJ Ready Red, and Willie D.
Photo by Betty Tichich/© *Houston Chronicle*. Used with permission.

I. Playing Different Games

By age eight, Prince was making a few dollars here and there by cutting neighborhood lawns and selling the birds he'd illegally hunt in the city. As an adult, he found employment hawking glitzy cars and working in a bank, among other hustles. But changing the course of music history is hard to do when you're locked down from nine to five. Self-employment was destined to be the path for the ambitious entrepreneur. The label Rap-A-Lot was started. Among Prince's goals was to make enough money to buy his mother a house of her own.

Hitting the height of its powers just as Jordan, Magic, and Barkley were breezing past the rest of the world's best at the 1992 Barcelona Olympics, Rap-A-Lot had its own dream team. It cultivated a new style, flavor, and ethos for the South to revel in. "Gumbo Funk" is what they called it. And the hits kept on coming.

"Rap-A-Lot was known for taking risks," says Big Mike, a one-time member of the Geto Boys who went on to cut some solo records for the label. "We were making the music and putting out what we felt we wanted to put out. J. Prince, he had a vision at the time for the label—what he wanted the sound to be like and what he wanted to be recognized for."

Rap-A-Lot begins with Sir Rap-A-Lot. It was 1986, the year of the destructive Hurricane Bonnie, Houston native Kenny Rogers's country hit "Tomb of the Unknown Love," and *The Texas Chainsaw Massacre 2*. The young rapper, along with friends Raheem and Sire Jukebox, would skip school, trade raps, and dream big. So Sir Rap-A-Lot's older brother, James Prince, made the trio a deal: "Go to school; I'll support you in rap."

"They put me in a position where I had to honor my word, because every day after school they would show up at my grandmother's house and be performing on the porch," Prince told *Complex*'s Rob Kenner in 2011. "So grandmother would call me and say, 'You got these boys over here.' So I had to honor my word."

Sir Rap-A-Lot, Raheem, and Sire Jukebox became the first iteration of Prince's greatest design: The Ghetto Boys (which would later evolve into Geto Boys). The first release credited to the group, "Car Freaks," drew heavily from path-finding Queens trio Run-DMC, even down to a shout-out to Adidas. Houston, though, was ready to embrace some of its own.

(above) (left to right) Rap-A-Lot founder and CEO James Prince ("Jay") and Geto Boys' Akshen aka Scarface; Public Enemy's Chuck D and Professor Griff; Geto Boys' Bushwick Bill and Ready Red (Willie D, with back turned, is cropped out of photo.) Photo courtesy of Ready Red. *(opposite)* The Ghetto Boys' debut single, "Car Freak" (RAP-777), from 1987, with the original lineup: (left to right) Oscar Ceres aka Raheem, Thelton Polk aka K-9, and Keith Rogers aka Juke Box (later Sire Jukebox).

(*above*) The Ghetto Boys' second single, 1987's "You Ain't Nothing" b/w "I Run This" (RAP-779). (left to right) Prince Johny C, Grand Wizard DJ Ready Red (on hood), and the Undisputed Sire Jukebox (sitting). (*opposite*) The Ghetto Boys' third single, 1988's "Be Down" b/w "My Musician" and "Why Do We Live This Way" (RAP-50). (left to right) Grand Wizard Ready Red (standing), Jukebox, Bushwick Bill, and Prince Johny C.

The Ghetto Boys released their debut album, *Making Trouble*, in 1988. By now, the group consisted of rappers Sire Jukebox and Prince Johnny C, diminutive hype man Bushwick Bill, and DJ Ready Red, a producer out of Trenton, New Jersey, who J. Prince approached after seeing him win a DJ competition in Houston. Red had come up under the mentorship of Instant Funk's Raymond Earl and under the influence of Grandmaster Flash. Again, the record looked way to the East, with everything from the commanding cadences to the gold chains and black fedoras, which the group donned on the cover, nodding again to Run-DMC.

Diluting *Making Trouble*'s rock-rap flavor, though, were the frequent references to the 1983 movie *Scarface*. Lines of dialogue snatched from Al Pacino's coked-out Cuban crime lord were embedded throughout. According to DJ Ready Red, that layer came about one night in the studio, when he and Bushwick Bill were watching the flick as the producer played around with his drum machines.

Red remembers, "I'm watching *Scarface* and [Bushwick] sits down on the start-stop right around the time [the character] Sosa says, 'Hey, Tony, how do I know you're not a *chivato*?' And Tony Montana says, 'All I have in this world…' and it came in on beat. So I said, 'Oh shit, I'm on to something.'" That song became "Balls and My Word." A thousand rapping Pacino fans would draw from the same holy text.

To be making original rap music in Houston was a trailblazing effort. The city drew from the East Coast for its flavor, because, in lieu of their own heroes, that was the stuff people craved. "New York rap was the big scene in my neighborhood," says Andre "007" Barnes, who would go on to form one-third of Rap-A-Lot group 5th Ward Boyz. "The Geto Boys were a different thing. It was a big thing to see someone from our neighborhood [rap], because hip-hop was nearly just all New York rappers. So we really took pride in having someone from our neighborhood do it."

"There was an affinity for it because they spoke a different language," adds Marketta Rodriguez, who since 1991 has owned and operated the Serious Sounds record store on Houston's Martin Luther King Boulevard. "You had NWA on the West Coast, and you had Boogie Down Productions on the East Coast—everybody was speaking specifically to their region. Rap-A-Lot comes along and they're doing the exact same thing, whether they're throwing something in their raps identifying a local establishment… It was that local pride."

With *Making Trouble* receiving little national attention, J. Prince shuffled the deck. Sire Jukebox and Prince Johnny C left when, according to Red, plans were revealed to turn the Ghetto Boys into a more concrete gangster-rap outfit. A new lineup was put together with the inclusion of two aspiring solo artists: Willie D, another Fifth Ward survivor who eschewed a promising boxing career to try to make it in rap, and Brad

The Ghetto Boys in 1987: (left to right) DJ Ready Red (on hood), Sire Jukebox (sitting), and Prince Johny C. Photo via Michael Ochs Archives/Getty Images/Stringer.

(*above*) The Ghetto Boys' debut longplayer album, 1988's *Making Trouble* (RAP-100). (left to right) DJ Ready Red, Bushwick Bill, Sire Jukebox, and Prince Johny C.
(*opposite top*) The Ghetto Boys' sophomore album (never appearing on vinyl), 1989's *Grip It! On That Other Level* (RAP-103). The new lineup represents the now-iconic group of (left to right) Willie Dee (aka Willie D), DJ Akshen (aka Scarface), Bushwick Bill, and DJ Ready Red.

Terrence Jordan, who, when urged by Red, dropped his previous guise of DJ Akshen to take on the blood-soaked cloak of Scarface.

J. Prince now had his Julius Caesar. Scarface was a lyrical genius with an alien flow. He captured the grim side of Houston with Technicolor detail and wouldn't flinch when it was time to drop an enemy on his head. Jordan proved to be both the military brain and heavy artillery in Rap-A-Lot's arsenal. All the label needed was a plan for deployment.

The all-new Ghetto Boys recorded their 1989 album, *Grip It! On That Other Level*, a colossal step forward towards the street-level style that would define the group, yet not quite the Southern sound that would soon emerge from Rap-A-Lot. The up-tempo, sample-heavy offering (Curtis Mayfield, James Brown, Kool and the Gang, Steve Miller Band, among others) sounded like a hybrid of New York rap and NWA.

Grip It! attracted the attention of producer and Def Jam cofounder Rick Rubin, who signed the group to his new Def American label, changed their name to Geto Boys, and a released a revamped version of *Grip It!* as a new self-titled album in 1990. But mother company Geffen Records pulled support for the album because of a dispute over the lyrical content, specifically the Bushwick Bill's tale of rape and murder on "Mind of a Lunatic." Prince called out the company for racism. Geffen said the record's depiction of violence against women was something they could not stand behind.

"If people believe that the Geto Boys really do stuff like on 'Mind of a Lunatic,' they must also believe there's a real Freddy Krueger and a real Michael Myers," Bushwick Bill told writer Frank Owen for the November 1990 issue of *Spin*. Rick Rubin added, "I just wish [Geffen] understood that I'm proud of this piece of art and that's a valid reason to put it out, regardless of what they think of this record." Rubin would go on to secure alternative distribution with Warner.

The group's success caused fractures to appear. DJ Ready Red speaks of his bitterness about not getting what he felt he was owed, claiming the actual number of records the group sold were airbrushed to withhold money from them. Red left the group during the making of 1991's *We Can't Be Stopped*. None of his work on the record was credited.

"I had no problem with the Geto Boys; my whole beef was with Rap-A-Lot Records," says Red. "You have to pay your artists. I know money was being made." Accusations surrounding his business practices became a theme of Prince's career.

Before absconding, Red did turn in the beat for "Mind Playing Tricks on Me." The song encapsulates the Geto Boys' mastery. Red loops a rickety guitar line taken from Isaac Hayes's "Hung Up on My Baby" as the three MCs lay out the mental strain of ghetto living. Scarface ponders suicide. Willie D shakes as he reaches for his pistol. A hallucinating Bushwick smashes his fists against the concrete pavement. The beat is pretty but gritty; the wordplay cuts like a knife to the solar plexus. In the world of gangster rap, realness is a valuable commodity. Geto Boys were bringing raw pain at its most graphic.

"We were only holding a mirror up to things that we had lived through in our surroundings, which are the same [things] that exist in ghettos around the world," J. Prince told NPR in 2012. "So it was easy for people to embrace our subject matter."

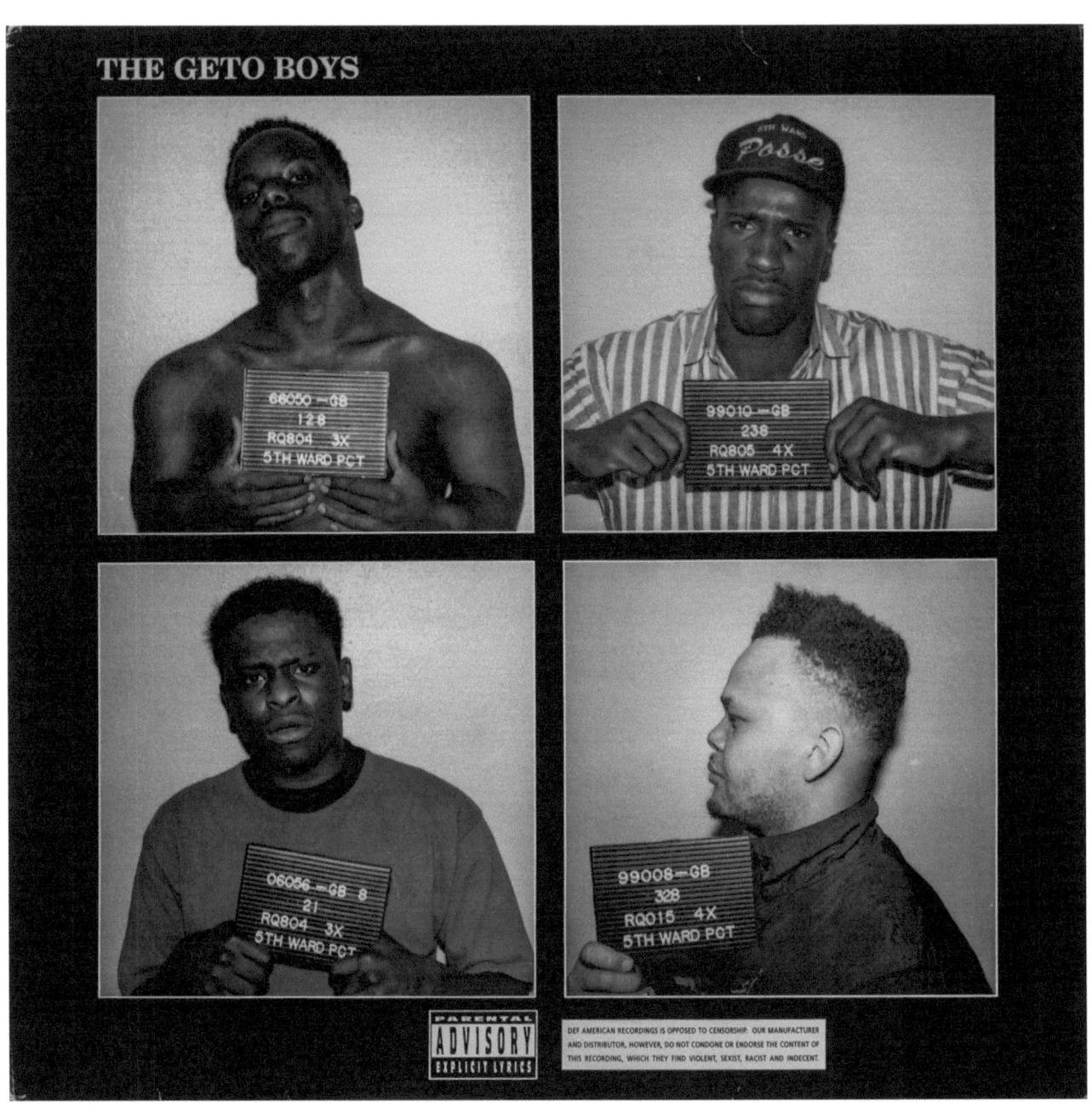

(above) The newly christened Geto Boys revamped their previous album, *Grip It!*, with the help of producer Rick Rubin, who signed the group to Def American. The result was 1990's self-titled *The Geto Boys* (DEF 24306). (counterclockwise from top) Bushwick Bill, Willie Dee (aka Willie D), DJ Ready Red, and Akshen (aka Scarface).
(opposite) Geto Boys' *We Can't Be Stopped* (Rap-A-Lot/Priority Records SL 57161), from 1991. The iconic album cover photo featured Willie D and Scarface pushing Bushwick Bill on a gurney in the hospital. Bill had just shot out his own eye during an argument with his girlfriend.

II. Damn It Feels Good

By the early '90s, hip-hop's golden age was in full flow. Both coasts were leveling up their production, wordplay, lyrics, and, as a consequence, their cultural influence. In the South, just as much inventiveness was being shown, with Rap-A-Lot positioned at the forefront of the region's scintillating scene.

With DJ Ready Red having permanently departed the label, someone needed to carry the weight. New Orleans producer Joseph Johnson—better known as N.O. Joe—had made his bones in New York, working with DeVante Swing on the first Jodeci album, among other projects. But a chance meeting with Scarface and his hype man, Big Mello, in a record store back in his hometown changed the trajectory of Southern hip-hop forever.

What followed must have resembled a scene out of Martin Scorsese's *The King of Comedy*. Johnson had been a Scarface superfan, even tailoring beats for the MC long before they ever shared a studio. So Joe made him a deal: come out to his car and listen to his beats. If he didn't like what he heard in the first ten to fifteen seconds, he was free to go. "That's how confident I was about the music," says Johnson.

The pair gelled and N.O. Joe was invited to Houston, where he hoped to contribute a couple of beats to the Geto Boys' new record, *Till Death Do Us Part*—an album that saw another New Orleans native, Big Mike, temporarily replace Willie D in the booth. Instead, Johnson produced eleven tracks and established the archetype for a rush of classics that would follow for the label. The guitar lines dripped with the spirit of the blues. The church organs were mournful. Johnson's beats were thick, grubby slabs of soul. The tracks had a lot more bottom than what had come before.

"I wanted to push the envelope as far as the sound, because I didn't feel like, as far as sonically, the records just didn't have that knock like New York," says Joe. "When I came to Rap-A-Lot, my vision was to bridge East Coast drums to like a Southern bass. But not like an 808 *boom boom*, just more of a knock in your trunk."

Rap-A-Lot's squad was small and compact. Most of the beats were made by N.O. Joe and John Bido, a long-time label knob-twiddler whose résumé includes Geto Boys' 1992 classic single "Damn It Feels Good to Be a Gangsta." Instrumentalist Mike Dean added some live licks to a lot of the orchestration. J. Prince still oversaw everything.

"[Prince] was really involved on the records and making sure that subject lines was on point, and made sure that all of the business was taken care of and certain things was promoted," reveals N.O. Joe. "That was his baby. That's what I felt from him. These projects were his baby."

According to Big Mike—who released his solo debut *Somethin' Serious* in 1994—the atmosphere throughout the label

was, at the time, like a family: "We knew we were making some vibes. Everybody was optimistic. We had a family over there. I did feel a sense of family at Rap-A-Lot. We were working pretty hard, man. We had a lot of artists on the label that didn't make it too big, but they still played a part with what we were doing. Yeah, I felt a sense of family over there at Rap-A-Lot during that time."

The label got on a roll. The Odd Squad—comprising of Devin the Dude, Jugg Mugg, and Rob Quest—made wacky rap you could spark a blunt to. And 5th Ward Boyz cut gangster funk that slapped you across the face. Ganksta N-I-P, Too Much Trouble, Choice, DMG, Big Mello, and others brought their own flavors. After dropping two solo albums—1991's *Mr. Scarface Is Back* and 1993's *The World Is Yours*—Scarface further established himself as a Southern deity on his third album, 1994's *The Diary*, which had productions by N.O. Joe and Mike Dean, and contained Face's first Top 40 hit, "I Seen a Man Die."

The studio was all business. Fun was had, and a little weed was smoked. In the case of the Odd Squad, a lot of weed was smoked. But alcohol and groupies generally weren't seen. During one session, the squad got competitive over one of Joe's beats, each trying to claim it for themselves. Prince was forced to step in.

Andre "007" Barnes of 5th Ward Boyz remembers: "Everybody wanted that track. J. [Prince] was like, 'Don't nobody own a track. You have to battle for this track if you want it.' So we all got in this one room. It was me, 5th Ward Boyz, Geto Boys, Scarface, Big Mike; everybody battled for the track. And we won the track. Everybody voted and we sounded better."

(top) Geto Boys' 1993 album *Till Death Do Us Part* (P1 57191) saw the new lineup of Scarface, Big Mike, and Bushwick Bill. *(opposite)* Rap-A-Lot Records promo photo of Scarface going solo. Photo by Sheila Pree.

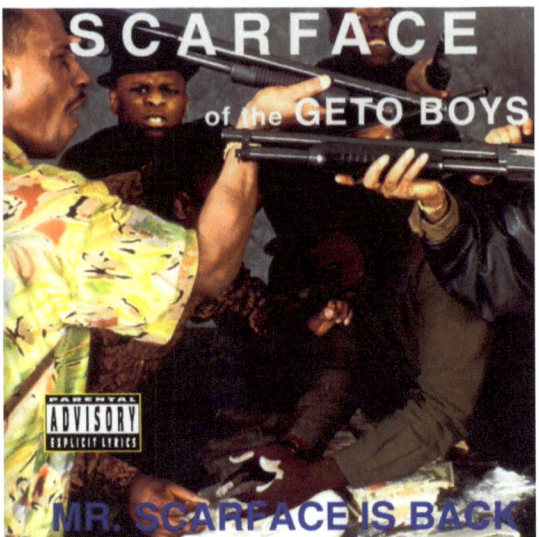

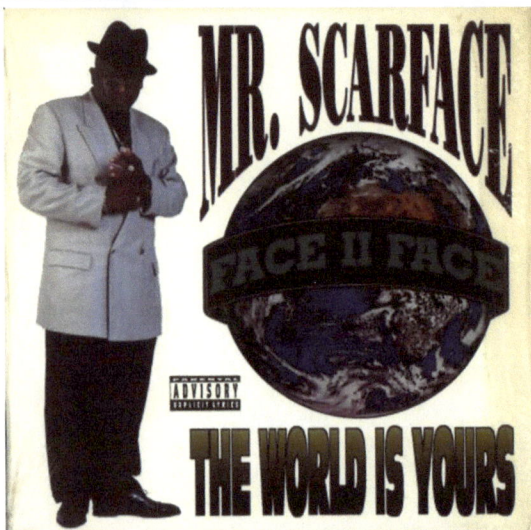

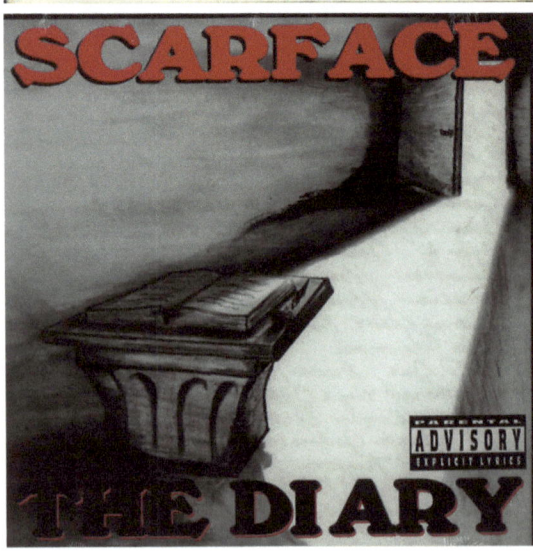

Even though the group didn't actually end up recording over that beat, their victory helped make the teenage group's mark in the corridors of Rap-A-Lot. "After that day, that's when [our first] album started," says Barnes, who alongside Eric "E-Rock" Taylor and Richard "Lo Life" Nash, made up one-third of the Phillis Wheatley High School–formed group. "We started getting beats from people, and they were like, 'Oh man, we didn't know y'all we're that good.' We started getting tracks. When we started that album, it was a great album because Scarface, Bushwick, everybody was around lending a hand, giving advice," he says of the 5th Ward Boyz' 1993 debut album *Ghetto Dope*. "It was magical."

But such magic can only be bottled all too briefly before it becomes diluted. No single moment or date I can pin down caused Rap-A-Lot's wave to break. There's been no major crash-landing to Earth—no steep fall to balance the label's rise. Unhappy artists, new faces, changing goals, and a shifting industry have all contributed to breaking the spell. Everyone I speak to agrees: at some point, things just started to feel different.

"Of course, they had newer producers come in, which was a good thing; there's nothing wrong with that," says N.O. Joe. "I think if we still had the foundation and then still brought in new people, it would still be on top of its game today. I think the separation of everybody doing other things or whatever, that's why it dissipated. I just wish towards the end there was unity with everybody coming together to do music for a greater cause. But as we get older, you have families, we have different goals in life, and that's just the way it is."

Geto Boys continued to release albums as a group and as solo artists throughout the late '90s and into the 2000s, but Scarface's relationship with J. Prince poisoned. In a 2015 interview with Noisey, the rapper claimed to dislike every Geto Boys album ever, and called out Prince for packaging and releasing his 2006 solo record *My Homies, Part 2* behind his back: "I feel like he was trying to ruin my career with cut-away material that never ever made the album. Just a totally disrespectful dude when it came to your shit. J didn't give a fuck about you, he gave a fuck about him."

Big Mike would also have a falling out with Prince, and went to prison after attempting to burn down Rap-A-Lot's studio and headquarters.

Other rumors have continued to dog Prince. Famously, there was a twelve-year investigation conducted by the DEA into Rap-A-Lot and its founder for involvement in drug distribution. The probe was canned in 2000. As reported by MTV, rumors spread that the case had been withdrawn after Prince supposedly donated $200,000 to then Vice President Al Gore's unsuccessful presidential campaign. Government officials and Rap-A-Lot have denied the claim.

By the mid-noughties, Southern rap was the hottest sound in hip-hop. No Limit and Cash Money were established

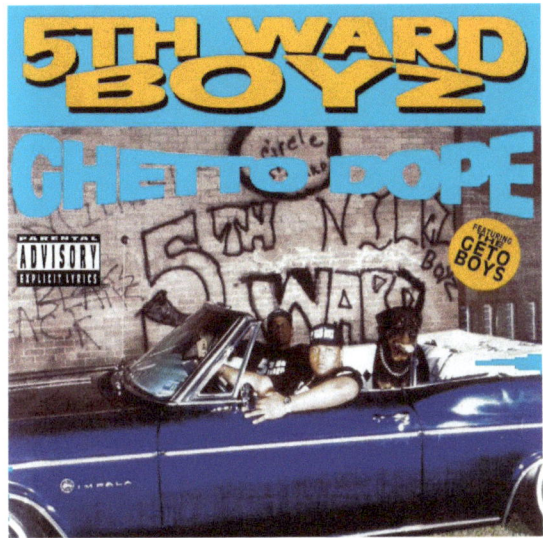

shortly after Rap-A-Lot, with both labels building their own indomitable legacy. Artists like Lil Wayne, T.I., OutKast, Young Jeezy, and Ludacris took the South to the highest peaks of rap stardom. For their part, Rap-A-Lot never wavered from its core tenets.

"Rap-A-Lot probably stayed true to its hard-core reputation more so that the other ones," says Marketta Rodriguez. "I'm thinking about Master P; he came along with No Limit Records. They started to cater towards the mainstream. Rap-A-Lot over all these years, even with their most recent release, Z-Ro, it still maintains its hard-core, in-your-face street sensibility."

Despite some latter-day successes with Z-Ro, Juvenile, and dropping solo records from UGK members Bun B and Pimp C (some of the latter's posthumously), the label's once prolific output slowed as Prince's interest in music waned. "This whole game right now is a game that I'm not that excited about anymore because of the new structure and all these different ways of being able to get music without paying," he told NPR in 2012. "It kind of kills my spirit from an entrepreneurial perspective."

Prince crossed into boxing promoting. Mike Dean's speed dial includes everyone from Kanye West and Sky Ferreira to Houston's own Beyoncé. In 2015, Scarface reignited his working relationship with N.O. Joe to record his first solo album in seven years. *Deeply Rooted* dropped on Facemob Music to positive reviews. "When it came out, everybody loved that record," says Joe. "And to both of us after these years and just him being independent, it was a great thing, because we still have that chemistry together."

Rap-A-Lot is still around; the company's latest release at time of writing being a Bun B compilation. The current roster is unclear, the harvest has slowed, and expectations aren't what they once were. But as long as there are old Geto Boys' CDs for dashboards to spin, Houston's concrete asphalts will forever flow under our tires. ⭕

Collins Adams Leysath, aka DJ Ready Red, sadly passed away after contributing to this article. He was fifty-three years old. Wax Poetics offers its warmest condolences to his family and friends.

Where I'm From

With their Grammy-winning debut album, 1993's *Reachin'*, Digable Planets introduced the masses to meticulously crafted jazz beats and playful lyricism about an insect hivemind, a sly metaphor for Black consciousness and communalism. But their well-thought-out sophomore release, *Blowout Comb*, stripped the allegory and plainly laid out their collective influences—from the Black Panthers to Islamic culture to Brooklyn's refound Afrocentrism—letting folks know where they're *really* from.

by A. D. Amorosi

Ishmael "Butterfly" Butler is doing Shabazz Palaces. Craig "Doodlebug" Irving is doing Cee Knowledge and the Cosmic Funk Orchestra. MaryAnn "Ladybug Mecca" Vieira is doing her solo thing with occasional guest shots. And together, Digable Planets is doing its thing as a touring unit, as they will February 2020.

"There was a plan to do new music, at first," says Butler, the instigator behind all things Digable since 1987. "Me and Cee get along. We're cool. For me, though, music is about passion and love. If you're not really getting along with a person, it won't work," he says of some sort of roadblock to new Digable Planets sounds. He never says why. "It's too intimate. And with music, making all music, there's too much of a high, an exaltation, a ceremony of joy to do it just to do it. So I don't think so."

Everyone admits though that anything is possible. It is that premise that drove three hip-hop artists with separate interests and ties to Black consciousness in their youth—from Seattle, Philadelphia, and Silver Springs, Maryland—to work together on Butler's concept of insect-based communalism, make it jazzy, and miraculously find a mainstream audience for its first album, 1993's *Reachin' (A New Refutation of Time and Space)*. It is that premise that made the Digable trio, after winning a Grammy for Best Rap Performance by a Duo or Group, consider their political/cultural polemic, turn it into a block party based on their new home, Brooklyn, and record the powerful *Blowout Comb* in 1994, only to break up months later by 1995.

(*opposite*) Digable Planets in 1994. EMI/Pendulum Records promo photo by Daniela Federici.

"Looking back at Digable is like looking back at pictures of yourself in high school and the clothes you had on—you thought you were cool, but you wouldn't think of wearing some of those outfits now," says Vieira.

Anything is possible; including a twenty-fifth anniversary celebration of *Blowout Comb* starting in winter 2020, to go with the Light in the Attic label's 2013 vinyl reissue.

For as richly dynamic that *Reachin'* may be in terms of its acid jazzy vibe, hop-pop reach ("We didn't intend for it to be commercial," says Vieira), and jovial melodicism, *Blowout Comb* is a misunderstood masterpiece, a deeply personal and epically social work referencing the Five Percent Nation, the Black Panther movement, Islam, Black Guerrilla Family founder George Jackson, and the then-bourgeoning Afrocentrism of Brooklyn in the 1990s. Not exactly eschewing jazz this round, but lending their usual brand of bop a darker funk patina. Rather than feature the lush, loud Boho harmonies of *Reachin'*, *Blowout Comb* is less hook-y, and its mellifluous voices and vocals are forceful yet buried deep within producer Dave Darlington's mix so to force the listener to focus on their idealism and abstraction.

"Both of our albums are our children, where you really can't pick a favorite," says Irving with a laugh. "I love them both. They affect my heart in two different ways—they were two different sets of times, generating two different sorts of excitement. But, yeah, *Blowout Comb* is stronger. More us."

Becoming the "us" that is Digable Planets started with Butler going back and forth from Seattle to New York City to Philadelphia in the late '80s, while interning at Sleeping Bag Records in NYC, and hanging onto a new vision of communalism based around insect iconography.

"Yeah, there were lots of references to bugs by my way of thinking," says Butler of developing the Digable Planets insect theology. "I was coming out of being raised by my mom and pop—Black Panthers, Marxists, Socialists, idealists that they were—and was always told, growing up, that I was part of a community, one larger than just myself."

From there, the young Butler built a system of metaphor, one where insects were organisms that never saw themselves as individuals, but rather something bigger, and would espouse a righteous, musical system, of beliefs. "Insects were always working for the good of this larger idea. The group. So would we. That is where my philosophy for Digable Planets came from. That is where having our names came from. The insect theory was a communal one."

Vieira and Irving held similar beliefs to that of Butler, but spoke different languages and had their own approaches. "My interpretation of that was that it was one for all and all for one," notes Vieira. "Ish's whole insect idea wasn't about ego; it was about instinct, doing what you do best to help

the hive.

Irving continued that thought by stating that the hip-hop hive mind-set was imbedded in him from his own father who was well versed in African American Socialism and Black Nationalist literature. "I knew about that community and that communalism. Those ideas weren't foreign to me, so when Ish brought it up in the form of insect logic, I definitely reacted to it positively."

Oddly enough, the "we" that was Digable Planets, at first, wasn't Vieira or Irving, but, rather another set of Digable insects.

"I had two other people I was working with in Seattle when I started the demos—another guy named Silkworm and another Ladybug, to be honest," says Butler, who had been woodshedding much of the material that wound up on *Reachin'* on his own, and with this initial trio. "At that time, Pendulum [the label run by Ruben Rodriguez] said they were going to sign me. Yet, from the time they *said* that, and the time they *did* that, three years had passed. So the other Digables went on with their lives."

Enter Irving through a family connection and a shared neighborhood. In Philly. As Butler's father was originally from the City of Brotherly Love, Ishmael's grandmother, uncles, and aunties stayed proud Philadelphians in the Mt. Airy section of the city. "Whenever I left Seattle, I'd go to Philly—my home base," says Butler.

That same neighborhood just happened to be where Irving's grandmother lived. "No, the grandmothers didn't know each other," says Irving with a big chuckle. "Now, that would have been weird."

Irving was, at that time, DJing, then rapping, with outfits such as the Osage Crew and the Dread Poets Society.

"I used to see Knowledge all the time," says Butler. "He was going to Howard University in D.C., but I would see him in Philly, this fly dynamic dude. He always had fresh clothes, fresh hair. *Who is this cat?* Then I found out he rapped."

(*above*) Digable Planets in 1993. Pendulum Records/ERG promo photo by Cathrine Wessel.

With that, Ish set out to make Craig a Digable. Butler tells of running into Irving at the Gallery—a Center City Philly mall space recently rechristened as Fashion District Philadelphia—where the former told the latter of the action happening around his Digable demos and the potential label deal.

"When I was with Dread Poets Society—DPS—we had a song called 'Skin Treatment,' which used that Art Blakey sample that we eventually brought to 'Cool like Dat,'" says Irving, referring to Blakey and his Jazz Messengers' muscular brass and reed extravaganza "Stretching" that would become the sampled center for Digables' eventual hit, "Rebirth of Cool."

Irving went on to say that when Butler heard "Skin Treatment," and the Blakey sample, he exclaims, "That joint is hot," before asking Irving permission to take that same track and use it for their Digable demo.

That enthusiasm came from Butler's own jazz roots, which dove deep. His father had a richly sophisticated ear when it came to the post-bop sounds of Lester Young, Hank Mobley, Sonny Rollins, and Coltrane, as well as the avant-garde free jazz of Eric Dolphy. Butler's dad also pushed the young Ish toward playing the saxophone. "My pop bought me an alto saxophone in middle school, and I spent my time in jazz band," says Butler. "I heard musical voicings through the saxophone at first."

Irving claimed that he thought Butler simply had the touch when he came to imaging sound, lyrics, and vision. "That was a genius mentality at work," he says.

While the two men of Digables formed a bond between Philly, NYC, and D.C., Irving knew too of a fellow Washington Howard attendee, Vieira, who then was better known for her dancing skills than for her rapping.

"I used to write down things in my head as a kid at home, but I never really rapped," states Vieira, while confessing to a love of jazz singers (e.g., Billie Holiday), and positive female hip-hop role models such as MC Lyte and Roxanne Shanté.

"Mec didn't really rap at first, so one night at Cee's

grandmom's house with a group of us doing our thing, we pushed her to rap," recalls Butler. "Funnily enough, her rap was strong and her flow was off beat. It was cool. Me and Cee were like, '*Dag.*'"

How dag? Vieira's rap eventually became "Nickle Bag of Funk" on the first Digables album.

Once united as the Digable Planets, Philly became a new home base for the trio as they recorded their demos in Northern Jersey.

"I was in awe of Philly," says Butler. "At that time, East Coast flavor was in full effect, and Philly had its own take on it. Schoolly D, Steady B. Philly was the next best thing to being in New York—Fifty-Second and Market. South Street, Germantown, South Philly, Penn Relays—that was the ultimate."

South Street became a real focus of the Digable Planets' then new universe when they hooked up with King Britt, the Ovum label co-owner, multi-genre artist, and DJ who eventually became part of their touring unit in 1992.

"I used to go to South Street where Britt was a buyer at Tower Records," laughs Butler. "I'd hangout in the hip-hop section, which was like three bins, and fantasized about having my own stuff for sale, all that kind of shit. King was there. A real unique-looking dude—had a flattop that was curled with different colors in it. He was a wild-looking dude. He was into house music too. When I had finished the new Digables demos in New York, I had one copy on a Maxell tape—and I needed to find somebody to make copies on a tape-to-tape dual cassette player. Nobody had those back in the day. I somehow knew that that dude had one…so I asked him if I could use it. After work, we met as his place near the Philly Art Museum, and he thought it would be huge. I never forgot that. After that, we became real friends. King taught me a lot about equipment and production."

Britt recalls Ishmael coming into Tower looking for 12-inch vinyl with tracks, "which were rare, so we started rapping about avant-garde jazz, which we had in common. I quickly pulled out a flyer for Silk City for Back 2 Basics, a hip-hop night I was doing at the time. He came through and we been friends ever since. He had the original demo for the album and came to the crib, where Josh Wink was my roommate, and made copies on my deck. I heard everything from demo to finished product. Actually, those demos are more like what Ish does now with Shabazz Palaces than anything else Digable. What Ish created was beyond anything I had heard at that point. It was on another plane than say Tribe or De La, whom I loved of course. It was like Herbie and Art Blakey, then Ish was the Sun Ra of it all. The Kafkaesque writing and references, this was on a whole other level. So I have always dug it…always."

Britt had already been a traveling DJ in Europe and the U.S. rave scene because of E-Culture (Britt and Wink's collaboration with a one-off single on Strictly Rhythm), so he was all about house and acid house. Between 1992 and the time when Digables opened for Sade on tour after *Reachin'* had dropped, Britt would become the Planets' touring DJ.

"I'm like the Fifth Beatle," says Britt with a chuckle. "Ish had been after me for a while to join the group initially. I was doing my house stuff and happy working at Tower and touring. I didn't really want to be in a band situation. So he kept on me and one day asked me to come up to meet with the label. They had to pretend to perform in front of Ruben Rodriguez so they could see what the whole group would look like—I had blond locks at this point—they were happy. I think that day I had to join for the first tour. I toured for two years and a few months on the Sade tour. One of the best experiences of my life. Also while on tour, I kept meeting all my house peeps, getting records, going to studios on our down time. Really crazy synchronicity."

Butler mentions this time and this sense of happiness as key to the Digables demeanor at that point, a period where they had recorded and mixed the first album between a studio in New York and a house in Bergen, New Jersey, a second floor above a dentist's office, with Mike Mangini and Shane "The Doctor" Faber. These two, between them, had mixing credits for Leaders of the New School, Run-DMC, and A Tribe Called Quest.

"We were totally comfortable with Mike and Shane, and we were over the moon with each other," says Irving.

"Shane's studio was just an apartment with a vocal booth in his closet, and still we were happy," says Vieira.

"This was the most beautiful time in time my life," says Butler. "You know how when you're a kid, and your mom and dad take you to their friends' house and there's a kid there—you never met him before—but by the time they're packing you up to leave, you're crying because you don't want to leave your new best friend? It was that kind of energy. We were living our dream together. It was the best. The relationships among the three of us was at its best. Everyone was waking up happy."

Signed with Pendulum Records in 1992, a deal that would eventually go through Elektra, the trio began recording songs for their debut album immediately. One of their earliest tracks would be that "Skin Treatment" treatment combined with another Butler cut, "Brown Baby Funk," a fusion retitled "Rebirth of Slick (Cool Like Dat)," that tied Butler's wonky jazz roots to Vieira's off-beat flow and Irving's funky street swagger. "Ishmael was the beat and the vibes—the genius," notes Irving. "I brought the street sensibility. Mecca brought the female balance—the yang to our yin. It was three people at the right time who were willing to compromise our egos and bend them to the will of the project, Ishmael's vision."

A hybrid was born—something jazzy, something hip-hoppy and something definitely poppy that crawled across the vibe of

(*opposite*) Digable Planets in 1994. EMI/Pendulum Records promo photo by Daniela Federici.

the entire *Reachin'* album come 1993.

Butler claims that there was no way that he could have predicted that the Digables sound and playful Afrocentric vision could ever be a hit. "We weren't operating for that standpoint; we had a hit because everybody like it. We were actually originally supposed to be marketed as a college act. There was actually another song that we and the label had a consensus that we thought might stand the best chance of being the first single. It had a George Duke sample, but we couldn't get the clearance. We had to go to 'Cool Like Dat' as our not-so-energetic choice. It wasn't what everybody wanted to do."

Released in November 1992, before the album's drop in the next new year, "Rebirth of Slick (Cool Like Dat)" peaked at #15 on *Billboard* singles chart and eventually won Best Rap Performance by a Duo or Group at the Grammys, beating out the likes of the then ragingly beloved Snoop Dogg/Dr. Dre pairing.

"Absolutely, they were hip-hop all the way through," notes Britt. "The whole process, in the studio, sampling, using jazz, technology, the beats, the rhymes, the attitude, all hip-hop all day. It's just that 'Cool Like Dat' became a pop culture phrase and phenomenon. Pop means popular, just popular hip-hop."

Their crossover success, a rarity at that time in hip-hop, however, made them suspect to purists of the genre who though they were too pop. "That bugged me, most definitely," says Butler. "Back then, there was no wanting to achieve crossover success. You could want that. So achieving it—no, it was not a good thing for us among the purists. The Grammy didn't help, especially since Snoop and Dre had it in the bag. But the event itself was a gala experience. Here, there was no reticence. Once you're there, you experience it a whole other way. We understood the magnitude of the moment, especially since the award shows were just starting to get into rap. It was amazing. [Jazz trumpeter] Clark Terry played with us. Bono was there, giving Old Blue Eyes a Lifetime Achievement award that night. It was amazing."

As good as things got for the Digables at that point, a harder reality had already begun to settle in. Vieira's mother was terminally ill during the Grammys time and into the recording of the next album. Pendulum was getting ready to switch distribution partners from Elektra to EMI Records, and a whole new crew of promotions people who didn't know the band. Butler and Irving felt as if they had to rally against the perceived notion of the Digables as a soft pop act, or just another cog in the Native Tongues movement.

"We wanted to bring clarity to where we were coming from in the first place," notes Butler, of taking the communal insect hive metaphor into that of his politicized Seattle upbringing—and that of his Planet-ary comrades—to the familiar world of the Black Panthers, the Five Percent Nation or the Nation of Gods and Earth, Islamic issues, and all forms of Black Nationalism.

No one was going to confuse the Daisy Age aspirations of *Reachin'* with stirring, funky new songs such as "Jettin'," where Ish raps, "My heroes died in prison, George Jackson." Or "Dog It" with its references to "making bacon" and bell hooks. Or the Blaxploitative "Dial 7 (Axioms of Creamy Spies)/NY 21 Theme" with its talk of "Che Guevara his young urban guerillas/ Sparks the revolution Black tactics, whatever."

Or the opening track, "The May 4th Movement Starring Doodlebug," with Ladybug's curt fluid verse leading the charge.

"One time for your mind/ Two times for Mumia, Sekou/ Three times for my Brooklyn dimes/ Seven times for pleasure/ I don't trip, I don't trip/ We don't trip, nah we don't trip/ We don't trip, please don't trip/ We don't trip, pleasure/ Now, 16 times for the mind thieves/ For my thinking Intel, I am Erica/ Counterfeits don't stop the wettest of us/ We Brooklyn we define the Black people equal to who, yeah/ What you supply/ I know when I know when I drop dip/ That was in beetle's but a snake try to spill a score/ On my pride I'm in my Cammy/ We bust at COINTELPRO we creamy like/ Fuck that, we Creamy Spies tell you scheme-y lies/ We let our creamy bullets fly/ Should it reflect the sun/ We say yes when we think of gettin' dipped/ We says guess say yo comrades rest."

Butler was pleased and proud that he and the Digables ("the first album was more Ish; the second was more about the three of us," notes Irving) would more directly reference the Black Conscious socio-politicism of their collective upbringing. So was Irving. "We most definitely wanted to reference that, open ourselves to that," Doodlebug says. "The second album had to be that, especially since we were also rallying against how we were perceived with the first album."

Mention the religious aspects of Islam to Irving and he says that it was Islamic culture, not religion, that fascinated him. "I grew up around Five Percenters, Muslims, Christians, gangsters, hustlers, nerds, athletes. I had people on my block who wanted to build things, people on my block who wanted to destroy things, people on my block who wanted to play basketball and baseball all day long. Everyone thought differently—my father was a Black Panther, we went to different universities and had unique intellectual pursuits—I was, however, the only one who represented Islam in a way that was pronounced."

Recording with Dave Darlington (Phyllis Hyman, Raekwon, Adeva) and living in the bourgeoning new Brooklyn, Butler said that the Digable were exposed to sounds and ideas far beyond their own impulses. With all that, the trio brought that B-lyn block party vibe to *Blowout Comb* as a funky result.

"Dave was the conductor," says Irving.

"We weren't living on to top of each other anymore," says Butler, who notes how he and Irving bunked together for a time when they first moved to the boroughs. "We were all taking care of ourselves and our children, living apart from each other, but only six blocks away from the other. The community was vibrant. Spike Lee was there doing his thing. Biggie was down

(opposite) Artwork from the inner sleeve of 1994's *Blowout Comb* (EMI/Pendulum Records).

the street. Gang Starr too. It was a fertile environment—all the music, art, and culture around every morning when you woke up and every night when you went to sleep. We were in the middle of that. It was a challenge to be around those talented people. You had to be original, you had to be steadfast. You had to be prolific. You had to be ready. People within that same community had a lot of feeling, at the time, for what hip-hop was. There was a lot of self-checking."

The music for *Blowout Comb* was wild, free, and strident, a large-scale Donald Byrd meets Parliament-Funkadelic production based in part on the ten-piece band that the Digables put together for their Sade opening tour slot. With Darlington behind the board, live instrumentation was recorded then looped and layered onto mounds of additional keyboard, percussion, and guitar, with wads of vintage samples coming from jazz-bos such as Wes Montgomery and Grant Green, funkateers like the Meters and soul stirrers such as Bobbi Humphrey and Roy Ayers.

"It took us about the same amount of time as the first album to record *Blowout Comb*, like four to five months, only this time we recorded like three times the amount of music," says Irving. "It was a whole other level of production."

The enormity of the production, as tight and orchestrated as it was, allowed for a looseness in its execution. "We were relaxed, but exacting. Specific," says Irving.

At the time of *Blowout Comb*'s release, Mecca told *SPIN*, of such specificity, that "it was time to be more direct on how we felt about things, and the need to assess them."

They were even more productive and specific when you consider that, before all of *Blowout Comb*'s writing and production, Ishmael Butler took a trip to the Los Angeles suburb of Watts where he hooked up with the elders of Black Nationalism, who introduced him to the Bloods and the Crips, to understand where the past of Afrocentrism met the present. "The photos from inside the *Blowout Comb* booklet came from that trip," says Butler. "Everything about that time had a profound effect on everything I did going into the album." Even Butler's Auntie Kathleen got in on the action as it was her collection of Emory Douglas drawings and Black Panther newspapers that became part of the album's packaging. "She was in the movement, and I thought all of those images, and that of the blowout comb, looked powerful together."

Britt recalls that Ishmael and the crew had always been about Black pride. "It's all on the first album too, but just not as in your face. With the crossover of the first album, the audiences were less Black than we wanted, and I feel out of frustration, they went a bit deeper and blatant with *Blowout Comb*. Look, my parents were all into the Panthers and Black Nationalism too, so I totally embraced what they were doing, but I left the group to start Ovum [label] and keep the Philly scene growing. But Ursula Rucker was our first record, so the word of Black Nationalism continued to be important."

One aspect of *Blowout Comb* where its sound met its vision was how Darlington and Butler obscured its lyrics and vocals behind layers of instrumentation. Rather than shout the Afrocentric purpose out loud, it was if Digable Planets was whispering so to make people pay closer attention. "That was my idea—have the vocals be an overall part of the mix," Butler says. "That made it more personal. Intimate. Even cryptic. Pulling it all off? That was Dave's job. He was a master at mixing and carving out space for sounds."

"I love how they created a lot of their own samples as well as using pre-existing samples," says King Britt. "The way it is mixed though is where it's at! Really dull on the top end, kind of like a mix tape, which accentuated the bottom end. Such an analog-sounding record."

No matter how adventurous or catchy in parts—"9th Wonder (Blackitolism)" was as fever-pitched, funky, and melodious a single as any from *Reachin'*—*Blowout Comb* went nowhere, a failure that didn't help the prevailing mood at Digable Planets' home base. Was it fair to say that its poor sales were a motivating factor in ending the band when it did? Or was it more?

Irving mentioned that Pendulum's move from Elektra to EMI left the Digables friendless on the label front. Personal problems within the band, and a dissolution of good feelings among them, pushed for a finale. "No, we won't say," states Irving. And no one did when asked.

"If it had been successful, we would have stayed together," says Butler. "It was cool us being on tour together, but I know that Cee and Ladybug had their own musical ideas. I guess when they saw something not being successful, I guess they thought why do this rather than fulfilling their own desires."

No matter. *Blowout Comb* was and is beloved by its makers, and wound up as a catalyst for everything each Digable did in its wake.

"After that album, I discovered rock—the Beatles, Pink Floyd—stuff I never heard as a kid," states Butler. "But between the avant-garde jazz that I loved growing up, and the music I made with *Blowout Comb*...that's what Shabazz Palaces is now. That album is quite an accomplishment." ⬤

DIGABLE PLANETS
Intercommunal Sound Service

VOLUME 1 © 1994 Pendulum Records

BLOWOUT COMB

King of New York

Frank White was already a seasoned photographer when in 1987 he fell into an opportunity with a fledgling hip-hop magazine called *Word Up!* In the years to come, White shot a who's who of New York's rap scene, cementing his own legacy as rap royalty behind the lens.

text and photos by Frank White

One day in the summer of 1986, I am watching MTV and a video comes on that featured one of my favorite rock bands of the 1970s—Aerosmith—that teamed up with one hip-hop's earliest and most influential group of the rap genre to perform one of Aerosmith's hit songs from their 1975 album *Toys in the Attic*—the song was "Walk This Way." Back then, to me, this did not seem to fit Aerosmith's style by getting a hip-hop group to put a spin on a major rock hit.

The video was filmed at the Park Theater in Union City, New Jersey. Just Steven Tyler and Joe Perry from the band were there to film along with all three members of Run-DMC. Tom Hamilton, Brad Whitford, and Joey Kramer of Aerosmith were not taking part in the video, so the rhythm guitarist, bassist, and drummer from the New York City glam band Smashed Gladys filled in as background musicians. Due to the fact that Aerosmith was not at the top of their game at that time, this remake of their song (by help of the video) revitalized the band's career. The resurgence in popularity of the music video and the fact that rap was starting to gain strength in music culture of the mid-1980s strongly helped out.

(*opposite*) DMC of Run-DMC at Madison Square Garden, August 17, 1987. Photo by Frank White.

One of the publishing companies that I was working with at the time owned *Hit Parader* and *Faces* music magazines and was located in River Edge, New Jersey, which was ten minutes from the town I lived in. I would go there often to sell my photos, dropping off and picking up used and unused slides and black-and-white prints.

I went there one day in the spring of 1987 and was asked by one of the editors if I wanted to photograph for a new magazine they were going to try out called *Word Up!* I was like, "*Word Up*, what does that mean?" After they told me, I became their first photographer for their new magazine. My first assignment was to shoot a press conferences with two New York City area rap artists, Run-DMC and Beastie Boys.

The day of the press conference, which was at a restaurant in midtown Manhattan, I made sure to get there early and got a front-row seat. There were a bunch of other photographers that showed up as well. Both groups had three members and were separated by a rep for the tour. We all shot photos of them just sitting there while being asked questions about the tour. After the sit-down press conference, we all went upstairs to a rooftop lounge to take more photos of both groups sitting together on the ledge of the building, and we took as many photos as possible within a few minutes; and then the event was over.

I did not know at that point what my next assignment would be. I get a call a few weeks later from the editor for the magazine; her name was Gerrie Summers. She asked me if I wanted to photograph the Run-DMC/Beastie Boys tour at Madison Square Garden, and I agreed to photograph my first rap concert.

(*above*) Beastie Boys and Run-DMC posing for rooftop photos for the press, spring 1987.
(*opposite*) Run-DMC and Beastie Boys at the press conference.

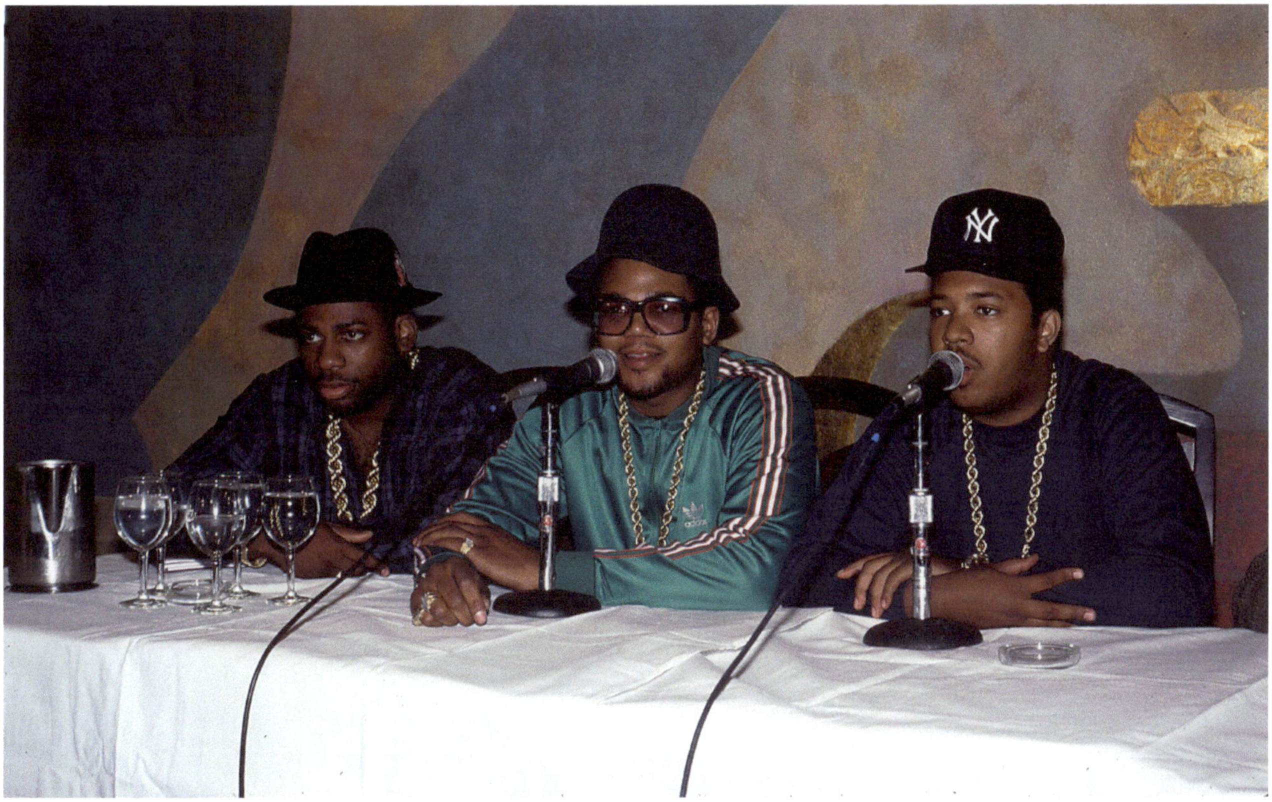

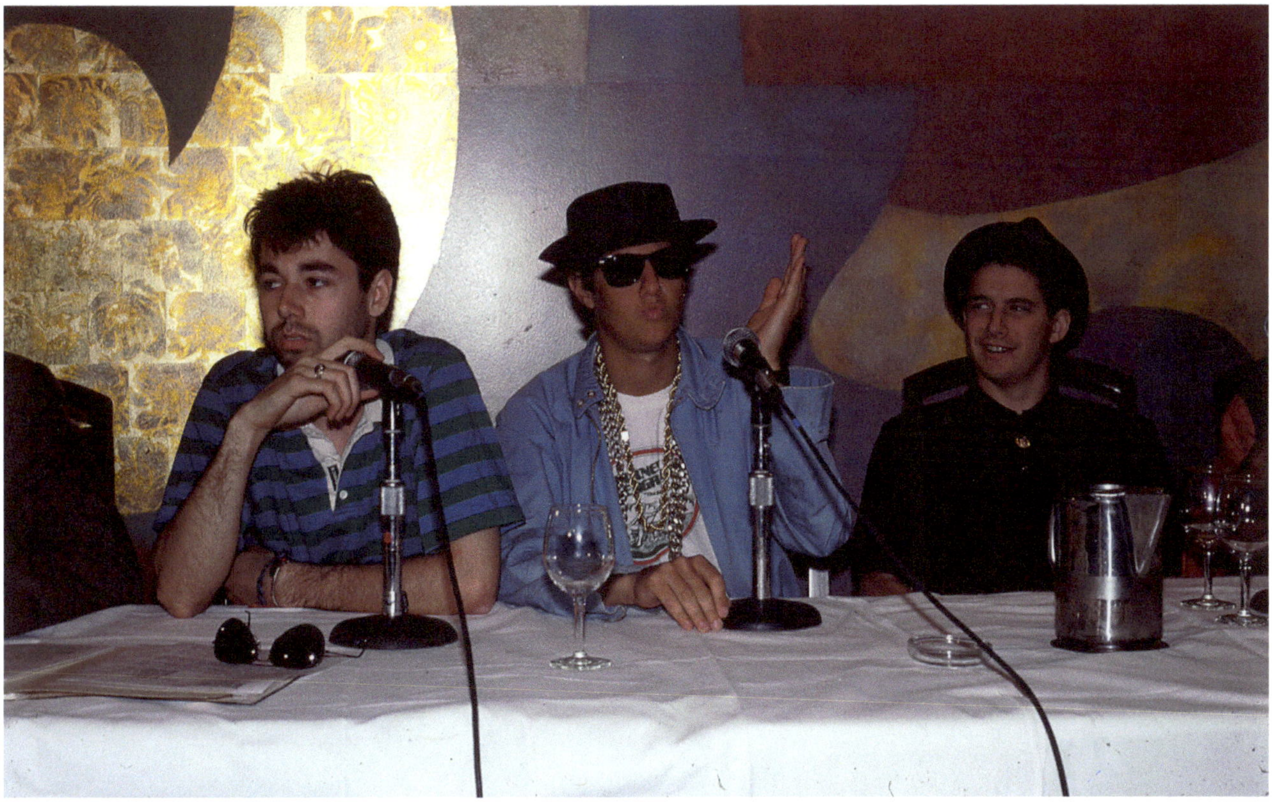

When I arrived at Madison Square Garden for the Together Forever tour on August 17, 1987, starring Run-DMC and Beastie Boys, there was a bigger police presence than the usual amount I would see at the rock, heavy metal, Southern rock, and R&B concerts I had attended at MSG over the last twelve years. I entered the Garden and had to go through this airport-style metal detector, and it felt like something was about to go down, and it certainly did.

The sold-out crowd of twenty thousand came to party, dance, and wave their arms in the air like they just don't care. The night started off as Davy DMX spun a few tunes to get the crowd warmed up. Then Run-DMC hit the stage dressed in black with Run (aka Joey Simmons) and DMC (aka Darryl McDaniels) with their trademark black hats and thick gold chains around their necks strutting their stuff around the stage, rapping songs off their latest album release with their DJ, Jam Master Jay (aka Jason Mizell), also dressed in black doing the spinning and scratching in a DJ tower booth behind Run and DMC. With the initials JMJ below him, Mizell got the crowd revved up by waving his arm back and fourth to get the crowd to do the same as the group blasted out their hit songs from the past few years that included "Hit It Run," "Sucker M.C's," "You Be Illin'," "My Adidas," and "Raising Hell." Then the rappers from Hollis, Queens, got their posse onstage along with the Beastie Boys for their encore song, "Walk This Way," and the crowd went crazy.

(opposite) The one and only Jam Master Jay (RIP). *(above)* Run and DMC having a blast at Madison Square Garden, August 17, 1987.

During the show, there was some excitement offstage as boxer Mike Tyson was in attendance and fans who noticed him were starting to gather round for photos and autographs. Tyson had to head backstage, where I was able to go with my photo pass and grab a few photos of him with another New Yorker, rapper LL Cool J, who had showed up backstage. Of course some backstage guests managed to get in a couple shots with the two champs.

After the Beastie Boys' personally designed stage curtain dropped, the group came out onstage dressed in T-shirts, jeans, sneakers, and hats, with two go-go girls on both sides of the stage dancing inside steel cages. A bar table was set up in the middle of the stage with a beverage Jug cooler and a blender, with friends mixing and pouring drinks and beer for Adam "MCA" Yauch, Michael "Mike D" Diamond, and Adam "Ad-Rock" Horovitz. Their DJ had his setup hanging from the rafters of the Garden.

The Boys got their headlined show off rapping to the crowd with songs like "No Sleep Till Brooklyn," "She's Crafty," "Slow and Low," "Rhymin' & Stealin'," "Posse in Effect," "Brass Monkey," and "Fight for Your Right" as they were chugging beers and drinks, letting some of it fly around the stage during the show. At one point, they would chase after a photographer and then another guy around the stage. While climbing platforms that were attached to the stage, they were having a blast while singing their brand of party songs all from their current album *Licensed to Ill*, giving the sold-out crowd a show that most or all of them never witnessed before. As the show was ending, I was able to leave before most of the fans left the arena; when I got outside, there were way more police surrounding the Garden in riot gear. I was able to get past them and got the hell outta there. A couple days later, I heard there were a few arrests, but it was a night that I would not forget.

(prior spread) DMC interacting with the audience. *(opposite)* DMC and Run strutting the stage. *(top)* LL Cool J getting his chain playfully yanked by prize fighter Mike Tyson. *(above)* Backstage fans crowd the two champs for a pic. Madison Square Garden, August 17, 1987.

(*above*) Mike D. (*opposite*) Ad-Rock. Madison Square Garden, August 17, 1987.

(*prior spread*) Ad-Rock and Mike D onstage at Madison Square Garden, August 17, 1987. (*above*) *Word Up!* magazine (#4) from February 1987.

The next day, I went to the Kodak plant in Fair Lawn, New Jersey, right down the road from *Word Up*'s office, where I had gotten my photos developed for years. I wanted to get the photos done quick, because the magazine was putting together the latest issue and were looking to put Run-DMC in the issue, as they were one of the hottest rap acts at the time.

I got the slide photos back a few hours later; I looked them over and saw some real nice ones and gave the art director at the magazine a selection of photos to consider. When that issue came out a couple weeks later, to my surprise, they ended up using one of my photos of Run-DMC sitting on the edge of the stage in front of me on a split cover with rap's hot solo artist LL Cool J. This helped fuel my desire to photograph more of these shows. In the next couple of months, the magazine assigned me to photograph top rap acts Public Enemy, LL Cool J, Stetsasonic, KRS-One, Eric B. and Rakim, Whodini, Fat Boys, as well as Whitney Houston. ⬤

Excerpted from the upcoming book *King of New York: My Years as a Hip-Hop Photographer for Word Up! Magazine* by Frank White, published by Wax Poetics Books. Coming in 2020.

(top right) Cover of the forthcoming book *King of New York* by Frank White (Wax Poetics Books). *(above)* *Word Up!* anniversary party in New York City, October 1988. All photos by Frank White.

www.ingramcontent.com/pod-product-compliance
Lightning Source LLC
Chambersburg PA
CBHW041958150426
43194CB00002B/53